THE METROPOLITAN COMMUNITY

ADVANCE PRAISE FOR

THE METROPOLITAN COMMUNITY

Partnering for Equality Across the Educational Divide

"Taines delivers a complex and hopeful answer to her question, "How do we get advantaged people—white and wealthier people—to contribute to inequality's un-making?" She demonstrates that the answer, although riddled with misrecognitions—begins by enabling privileged young people to "see" educational inequality and their stake in it—not to blame or burden them—but to invite them into activism alongside peers who find themselves disadvantaged by the inequality from which they benefit. This story of a city-suburban partnership, that is designed to do just that, makes evident how we can inspire and draw upon the power and agency of youth to help write a more just future."

Carla O'Connor, University Diversity and Social Transformation Professor and Arthur F. Thurnau Professor, Marsal Family School of Education, University of Michigan, Ann Arbor

"Americans sometimes claim to believe in equality, but you wouldn't know it by how they fund public education. In a deeply-researched study of metropolitan Chicago that compares a poorly-resourced city school with a wealthy one in the suburbs, Cynthia Taines uses her enormous skills as a sociologist to illuminate the systemic inequalities that plague the nation's schools. Taines does more than that. In sparkling prose, she tells a remarkable story about how a coalition of students from these two schools, with the support of dedicated teachers and community activists, lobbied legislators for more equitable public school funding in Illinois."

William J. Reese, Vilas Research Professor, Educational Policy Studies and History, University of Wisconsin, Madison

"At a time when education, equity, and democracy are under attack, Cynthia Taines provides us with a powerful story of young people working together across lines of race and class to create a more just public school system. The students in the Metropolitan Community Project study, discuss, and forge common cause to upend educational inequality–and this process uplifts them all."

John Rogers, Professor of Education and Associate Dean for Research and Public Scholarship, University of California, Los Angeles

THE METROPOLITAN COMMUNITY

Partnering for Equality Across the Educational Divide

BY

CYNTHIA TAINES

GORHAM, MAINE

Published by Myers Education Press, LLC
P.O. Box 424 Gorham, ME 04038

Myers Education Press is an academic publisher specializing in books, e-books, and digital content in the field of education. All of our books are subjected to a rigorous peer review process and produced in compliance with the standards of the Council on Library and Information Resources.

Library of Congress Cataloging-in-Publication Data available from Library of Congress.

13-digit ISBN 978-1-9755-0743-5 (paperback)
13-digit ISBN 978-1-9755-0744-2 (library networkable e-edition)
13-digit ISBN 978-1-9755-0745-9 (consumer e-edition)

Printed in the United States of America.

All first editions printed on acid-free paper that meets the American National Standards Institute Z39-48 standard.

Books published by Myers Education Press may be purchased at special quantity discount rates for groups, workshops, training organizations, and classroom usage. Please call our customer service department at 1-800-232-0223 for details.

Cover design by Amanda Weiss.
Cover art by Good Studio/Adobe Stock (people and puzzle) and zyxroun/Adobe Stock (school).

Visit us on the web at **www.myersedpress.com** to browse our complete list of titles.

Educational equality is basically like: Every student is going to be something, and every school will give that child whatever they need to become what they want to become.

—Janelle, Taylor High, Chicago

For the Metro students.

CONTENTS

Part I - An Introduction to Educational Inequality

Chapter 1 Introduction 3

Chapter 2 School Resources Lost & Found 19

Part II - Talking About Educational Inequality

Part II Introduction 43

Chapter 3 Communicating the Educational Divide: Wyndham 45

Chapter 4 Communicating the Educational Divide: Taylor 59

Part II Coda 77

Part III - Educational Activism

Chapter 5 The Students & the Legislators 91

Part III Coda 133

Part IV - Metro Student Outcomes

Part IV Introduction 141

Chapter 6 Personal Change: The Taylor students 143

Chapter 7 Personal Change: The Wyndham students 163

Part IV Coda 183

Part V - The Metropolitan Community

Chapter 8 Conclusion with Next Steps 191

Acknowledgments 205

Metro Directory 209

About the Author 213

Index 215

PART I

An Introduction to Educational Inequality

CHAPTER ONE

Introduction

School Funding & The Educational Divide

THE RESEARCH HAS FINALLY caught up to what any city student or teacher implicitly knows: school funding matters. Using recent, more advanced statistical techniques, and the capacity to make definitive causal connections, scholars in the past decade have been able to show that increasing school funding raises student achievement (Jackson et al., 2016; Jackson, 2020; LaFortune et al., 2018; Roy, 2011), increases high school graduation rates (Candeleria & Shores, 2019; Jackson et al., 2016; Jackson, 2020), boosts college enrollment and college degree attainment (Hyman, 2017), and supports higher wages and family income in adulthood (Jackson et al., 2016; Jackson, 2020; LaFortune et al., 2018). Putting more funding towards schools also reduces the things we don't want, such as dropping out of high school (Lee & Polacheck, 2018) and the chances of living in poverty later in life (Jackson et al., 2016; Jackson, 2020). The effects of greater school funding are especially strong for our most vulnerable low-income students (Candeleria & Shores, 2019; Jackson et al., 2016; Jackson, 2020; Lee & Polacheck, 2018). Encouragingly, substantial increases in school funding yield even more substantial gains, doing a lot to close achievement and attainment gaps with more advantaged peers (Jackson, 2016; Lee & Polacheck, 2018).

So we know funding is critical, but in metropolitan areas across the country, city and suburban students are not receiving it equitably. Outer-ring suburban school districts are frequently places with high concentrations of wealth and whiteness, and because school funding is primarily locally-sourced, these areas can raise bounteous amounts for the students within their borders (Baker et al., 2022; Knight et al., 2022; Lichter et al., 2023; Massey, 2008; Owens & Rich, 2023; Sosina & Weathers, 2019).

The borders were an intentional creation. In the early part of the 20th century, federal policymakers and local officials colluded on housing, banking, and transportation policies to create mostly white, affluent communities and keep families who did not match this profile out (Darling-Hammond, 2013; Jackson, 1985; Massey & Denton, 1993; Massey, 2008; McGhee, 2021; Orfield, 2013; Rothstein, 2017; Siegal-Hawley, 2016). While these policies are no longer officially active, the municipal and district boundary-lines created during this time are still there, and in many places are serving their original function: separating white and higher-income students into suburban schools and cordoning off public funds (Baker et al., 2022; Darling-Hammond, 2013; Massey, 2008; Orfield, 2013; Owens & Rich, 2023; Reardon & Owens, 2014; Rich & Owens, 2023; Ryan, 2010; Siegal-Hawley, 2016, Sosina & Weathers, 2019; Stroub & Richards, 2013).

Across the border, city school districts in our metro areas are struggling (Ryan, 2010; Siegal-Hawley, 2016). The students attending city, neighborhood public schools are primarily low-income, Black, Latino, and recent immigrants (Leone, 2020). Their families historically were excluded from government subsidies for housing and higher education, and they currently experience racism and economic marginalization (Massey & Denton, 1993; Massey, 2008; McGhee, 2021; Orfield, 2013; Rothstein, 2017; Siegal-Hawley, 2016). As a result, the majority of city parents do not have the wealth to cover what's needed, despite voluntarily taxing themselves at higher rates to try (Baker et al., 2020; Darling-Hammond, 2013; Massey, 2008). Because the funds aren't available, so many resources students say they'd love to have go missing—a swim team, dance classes, smaller classes, college help, and working computers.

There is a mismatch between the knowledge that school funding matters and the denial of these funds to the primarily Black, Latino, and low-income students who attend city schools. The knowledge is helpful, but if that was enough, a change would've happened long ago. What keeps unequal funding in place is not a misunderstanding of its existence or effects, but the politics of advantage and an apathy frozen by hopelessness (Massey, 2008; Orfield, 2013; Ryan, 2010).

The separateness of outlying suburbs presents white and wealthier families with a built-in logic to define "their schools" narrowly as within suburban borders (Massey, 2008). Separation draws the focus inward, towards making sure suburban schools have the best and latest of everything and defending the gains against perceived threats (Siegal-Hawley, 2016). Disconnection from the outside diminishes empathy for city schools and city students. With these mindsets, affluent, white parents use their connections and clout to ensure the public school system is working in their favor (Darling-Hammond, 2013; Massey, 2008).

And with money talking, legislators get pulled into suburban communities' orbit. The cost of running for office constricts the diversity of our political representatives—most don't share a background with city students or come up through city schools (Baker et al., 2020; Ryan, 2010). Their affinity for wealthy constituents, and unfamiliarity with under-resourced schools, results in policy decisions that protect and expand on suburban interests (Darling-Hammond, 2013; Ryan, 2010). If they're even proposed, bills that suggest the reform and redistribution of school funds are watered down, or more likely, don't have the votes to pass.

Growing up in a system like this, inequality can begin to feel normal (Orfield, 2013, pp. 50-1). A city resident may see the direct harm and wish things were different but also feel like that's how they've always been. A suburban resident may hear tangentially about the struggles of city schools and be sympathetic but believe there's nothing to be done. Even when people want change, the bigness of the problem and its long historical arc make it seem impossible. The "hopelessness immobilizes us" (Freire, 1998, p. 70).

A metropolitan coalition can offer a new politics and new hope (Ryan, 2010). Public school families in cities can bring crucial assets to this work: experience with the obstacles undermining city schools, a sense of urgency about change, and a history of community organizing (Oakes & Rogers, 2006; Warren & Mapp, 2011). Suburban school families can apply their political influence and testify to the benefits of well-resourced schools (Ryan, 2010; Siegal-Hawley, 2016). A city-suburban alliance amplifies power by combining each community's strengths and adding more voices to the fight (McGhee, 2021; Siegal-Hawley, 2016).

This is the first book to depict city and suburban students trying out this allyship idea in hopes of equalizing their schools' funding. Taylor High School, in Chicago, and Wyndham High School, in the suburbs, are situated on opposite ends of the educational divide.[1] Taylor's student body is mostly low-income and Latino; Wyndham's is mostly upper-income and white. A Taylor student gets thousands of dollars less for their education than a Wyndham student does, each year. And since resources follow the money,

Wyndham has far and above what's available to Taylor, in terms of electives, supplies, facilities, and support. But the Metropolitan Community Project starts first by emphasizing what these schools have in common: both public high schools, 15 miles apart, in the same region, county, and state. And then it seeks to introduce another commonality by connecting students from both of these places, together. Over a school year (and sometimes more), Wyndham and Taylor students get to know their two schools and each other, and advocate for change.

❖

Two High Schools

The story begins with two high schools. How they are alike: both public schools, in the same county, state, and country. How they are different: almost everything else. Just about any place with a city and a suburb has the same bone structure: of opportunity, resources, and kids, separated. Of schools so obviously unequal.

Wyndham High is a mix of old and modern, with carved stone towers built in the early 1900s and newer state-of-the-art additions. At any time of day there are teenagers standing in clumps by the front entrance or lounging on the grass with backpacks strewn. The doors are unlocked, and students come and go at will.

The school is surrounded by green-space—athletic fields and trees—with parking lots and tennis courts closer-in. It's huge: almost 3,000 students go there from several neighboring towns. Just beyond, on tree-lined, wide streets, are what passes for modest houses in the area, with front and backyards, and peaked roofs. Go a little farther though, and dwellings expand in dimension, until you get lakeside, where there are enormous mansions, sweeping grounds, and views of the water. There is a small downtown nearby, with boutiques, a coffee shop, and a train station. Bordering a busy street is a more ungainly shopping center, but the town prohibits most chain stores, to create a sightlier atmosphere.

Wyndham High is in the suburbs, north of Chicago. While there are suburbs that aren't as upscale as this one, affluent, outer-ring suburbs are a common slice of American life. For the high school here, there is $25,000 available to spend on each student every year. Community fundraisers and fees add even more. It costs a lot to live in this area, and it is historically segregated. Reflecting its surroundings, the school is 85% white and 96% middle- and upper-income.

Taylor High is just 25 minutes away. Its architecture also dates from the early 1900s, but it hasn't changed as much over time. From the front pavement the school rises up somewhat grandly, brick with white columns, its name engraved near the roofline. Strips of green lawn and some plantings border the long sides of the school, marked off by short fencing. Students are not allowed in there: they must stay in the cafeteria at lunch, and after school, security starts shooing kids away from the entrance.

Taylor's what's called a "neighborhood high school," the kind of school that serves the majority of low-income, Black, and Latino students in the city (Leone, 2020). There isn't a competitive application to get in, as there is for the few selective, high-profile schools in Chicago. Instead, it's open to anyone who lives in the neighborhood, and kids mostly walk or take the city bus. They need to be buzzed in, and there's a metal detector in the entryway.

About 800 students used to go through Taylor's doors each morning. But enrollments have been falling: from lack of district support for the school, the opening of nearby charters, and fewer kids living in Chicago as the city becomes more expensive. Which is hard, because in addition to being a public school in the city, its funds are limited by having fewer "per student" dollars.

Near the school are small wooden and brick houses, some owner-occupied, some split into apartments. There are large trees and narrow, car-lined streets; most places don't have garages. I cannot tell by looking, but the students say they need to be careful leaving for the day: there is street violence here, and some routes are safer than others. They should be home before dark. On a wider street two blocks away, there's a cell phone store, a party shop, and numerous food choices: a panadería smelling sweet every morning, arroz con gandules y lechón, empanadas with chimichurri, hot chips from the gas station by the bus stop.

Like the restaurants, local families trace their heritage to countries all over Latin America, some immigrating generations ago, some more recently. Many parents work multiple jobs, and their kids chip in to help. Since the student body is so localized, and the city so segregated, the school represents the neighborhood: it is 90% Latino and 97% low-income. Chicago Public Schools only has to report what it spends for students in the city on average, and that's $15,000 per year. Most school-watchers here believe that students going to neighborhood schools like Taylor are receiving much less than that.

So far, the outlines of Taylor and Wyndham may be familiar: it's separate and unequal education all over again. But the story goes somewhere new when young people from the two high schools become partners for change.

This book takes you on their journey. You'll be alongside them as they visit each other's schools for the first time: while they walk the hallways, sit at a classroom desk, and watch the lunch rush in the cafeteria. You'll eavesdrop on their conversations, just like I did. You'll feel the discomfort when they don't know what to say, and the energy when it starts to flow. When we get to the part with the politicians, you'll witness evasions and pretty words. You'll catch the students' enthusiasm for being part of the process.

The students told me that actually being there is what made the difference: their physical presence in these schools, their talks together in-person, their unity. Reading from a distance is not quite the same, but the book will bring you close. By showing you that cross-community action is possible, and imperfect. By offering some hope.

❖

Building a School Partnership

My path to creating the Taylor-Wyndham partnership was through history, a kind of 'what would have been.' I learned about a crucial turn, in the early 1970s, when the Supreme Court stopped the spread of school integration. It had been progressing with grassroots pressure and the Court's urging: from south to north, from surface compliance to in-depth plans. But then, in 1974's *Milliken v. Bradley*, suburban school districts got let off the hook: they were freed from participating in the integration of their city centers. Suburban residents had intentionally moved and separated themselves and built almost all-white schools. And now they could stay this way. City schools, which had become predominantly poor and of color, had no access to the equality of opportunity promised in the original *Brown v. Board* decision (1954). Thurgood Marshall pointed this out, and he would know. He'd argued that decision and was now a Supreme Court justice. But in this case, he was in the minority.

My chills moment came from reading Marshall's dissent, when he said we should not let a school district's boundary become society's "new dividing line" (*Milliken v. Bradley*, 1974, p. 805). Equal educational opportunity is a right, he argued, and to fulfill it, "the city . . . and its surrounding suburbs must be viewed as a single community" (p. 804). Marshall's name for this place was a "metropolitan community" (p. 804). That was over fifty years ago, but for me, it remains a mythical ideal. Reading that phrase, I said to myself, 'I wonder if we could build that.' I'm still wondering, but I have a few more insights now.

To try to build it, I asked Ms. Dorsey, a teacher who'd formerly worked at Taylor, if she'd join me.[2] She said yes and recruited one of her colleagues there. She also invited the community-based organization in the neighborhood, which she'd collaborated with on social justice curriculum. I'd previously taught an evening class for educators on the Wyndham campus and tapped in to that network. With life changes and job turnovers, we've had various people swap in and out, but our team's structure has always been: teachers at Taylor and Wyndham, an education organizer, and me (an education professor).[3]

That first summer, we assembled in Taylor's library and began with a sort of book club, discussing readings on racial and economic justice and clarifying our own identities and values. From there, we expanded to consider the intentions of our newly named Metropolitan Community Project. We sketched out the cycle of student meetings for the upcoming year. When school started in the fall, the teachers recruited from their classes and after-school clubs. Students volunteered to participate, and they still do, some for multiple years.

It fluctuates, but in any given year about 30 students participate in "Metro," evenly balanced between Taylor and Wyndham. The project's diversity comes from the combination of two very separate schools. For example, in the most recent year, our students were 51% Latino, 43% white, and 6% Asian American, but all of the white and Asian American students were from the suburbs, and all but one of the Latino students were from Chicago.

❖

A Year in the Metropolitan Community Project

We've patterned Metro on the rhythms of a school year. The kids are introduced in the fall. With a list of mysterious clues, and only their partners to turn to for help (no phones!), they set out on a scavenger hunt to break the ice. Upon return, and after the buzz dies down, we all agree on guidelines for communicating respectfully, curiously. These carry over to the interviews they do with each other about school, in Taylor-Wyndham pairs. There's a presentation on school funding, with time for q&a. Leaving, there are hugs and exchanges of whatever social media they're doing these days.

It's getting cooler out when the Taylor students meet to think about how to tell their story: what they love about their school, what their school needs. They brainstorm which classes, clubs, and places to put on their school tour. They do a practice-run and talk through how they'll explain each stop. Then they do it for real: the Wyndham students are here. The Taylor guides take them around in small groups. They listen in on classes in progress and pause in front of murals. There's a break for lunch, with food many of the Taylor kids grew up on, and then it's back out to see more of the school. The end of the day brings reflection. Questions from Wyndham on what they saw, answers from Taylor on what their school day is like. Spoken-word poetry, depicting Taylor kids' lives outside of school. Then the Wyndham students head home. The Taylor students stay in the library to think back on how the day has gone.

It's winter now, officially cold, and it's the Wyndham students' turn to plan. There are so many choices, and the school is so big, that we've asked them to pare the tour down to just the parts they regularly use. The Taylor students arrive, and the Wyndham students bring them all over the school. Afterwards comes a conversation to process Wyndham, which leads naturally to comparisons, since they've now seen both schools up close.

When we have time and budget for more field trips, we add community tours designed by the students, and lunches with families, in here.

It still feels like winter—it's the Midwest after all—but officially we're in spring. After seeing the gap, and meeting new kids, the Metro students want to do something. Ms. Isabel, the education organizer, facilitates a conversation on where to focus their change energy.[4] Local activists and allies drop in to help, discussing campaigns already in-progress or what's worked in the past. The students take these building blocks and decide together how they want to push for equal schools. We get trained up on strategy: practicing how to make a case, write a public letter, deal with the media, or get a signature.

Finally, it's warm out. Perfect weather for going door-to-door, in the suburbs and the city, gathering petitions to change the Constitution and make education a right. Or writing letters in the cool of a borrowed church to every single state legislator. For sweating through meetings in un-air conditioned offices, trying to get local representatives to commit. Or keeping school open late, so parents can hear a declaration of student rights. Year-to-year, these are the kinds of actions students take. Some of them are for movement-building, and some for policy-changing. All of them spark the kids' energy to stay with it, to keep trying until schools are equal.

With summer here, we hold a little closing ceremony. The students share-out what Metro means to them, while eating cupcakes or conchas. There are more hugs, among the goodbyes.

❖

School Funding Policy Explainer

This isn't difficult math, but just to highlight: the difference between a Wyndham and a Taylor student's education is more than $10,000 a year. The amount a Wyndham student gets above is almost as much as what's provided to a Taylor student in total. There is, at minimum, a $100,000 greater investment in the public school career of a single suburban student, kindergarten through grade 12. Combined with other kids, that racks up quickly: into supportive facilities, teachers, counselors, and social workers; science equipment, books, and plays; course electives and sports teams; etc.

To explain how this can even happen, I need to say more about how school funding works. Across the U.S., public school funds come from a mix of local, state, and federal sources. In most places, it's the local funds that are the make-or-break for schools (Baker, 2018; Darling-Hammond, 2013; Jackson, 2020; Knight et al., 2022; Sosina & Weathers, 2019). These come from property taxes raised within the school district, from homes and businesses. The greater the price of these properties, the more money that is raised for schools. In rural areas where houses are spread out, and there are few stores or prosperous farms, the money going towards schools is tight (Baker et al.,

2020). In cities with lower-income neighborhoods, out-of-business signs, and public tax-free museums, what's available for schools is also scarce (Baker, 2018; Darling-Hammond, 2013; Massey, 2008; Ryan, 2010; Siegal-Hawley, 2016). Adding to this scarcity, city officials steer funds to gentrifying and old-money neighborhoods, and marquee schools, leaving poorer schools even less well-off (Darling-Hammond, 2013; Knight et al., 2022). Meanwhile, suburban homes with large square footage and expensive land can yield great school bounty even if the property tax rate is lower, relatively speaking (Baker, 2018; Darling-Hammond, 2013; Massey, 2008; Orfield, 2013; Ryan, 2010; Siegal-Hawley, 2016; Sosina & Weathers, 2019).

The local scene makes such a big difference because state support for education can be limited, and the federal government has always contributed only a tiny sliver. Most schools lean heavily on the local community, but communities are unequally able to help (Baker, 2018). This is how we get enormous disparities in school funding between rural, urban, and suburban places.

It's a problem everywhere, because local funds now make up almost half of school funding nationally. It's a particular problem in the state where this book takes place, because Illinois' contribution is so small that it takes great amounts of local funding to secure a quality education, but not all cities and towns can supply what's needed (Baker, 2018; Farrie & Sciarra, 2021). On top of this, what's "needed" is different, depending on the students who go there. English language learners, students with disabilities, and low-income students all need additional resources to help them meet the challenges in their lives and succeed in school (Baker, 2018; Baker et al., 2022; Jackson, 2020; Knight et al., 2022; Owens, 2023). Yet, these very students are often segregated in communities where lower-wage jobs, rental apartments, foreclosed homes, and empty storefronts are more common. This creates a double-whammy, where the students who need more than average attend low-income schools that can only provide less. Or that's true for how we currently do things. We could do it differently. And we should.

❖

Underneath the Educational Divide

What I just told you is the policy storyline for how we get those differences. But there is a deeper thread, from our history and present, of racism and economic exclusion, that explains why the schools that get so much almost exactly overlay with the communities where white and upper-income people live (Baker, 2020; Baker et al., 2022; Knight et al., 2022; Massey, 2008; McGhee, 2021; Orfield, 2013; Owens & Rich, 2023; Ryan, 2010; Siegal-Hawley, 2016; Sosina & Weathers, 2019; Stroub & Richards, 2013). The exclusivity of suburbs was not an accident. Not so long ago, early 1900s, there were little outpost northern towns that prohibited people of color, sometimes with hateful signs, sometimes through hurtful words and violence (Llowen, 2018; Siegal-Hawley, 2016). Then came the policies that recruited and welcomed white families from the city: the banks helped with the mortgage, the feds laid out the freeways, the towns built the roads home (Jackson, 1985; Massey & Denton, 1993; McGhee, 2021; Orfield, 2013; Rothstein, 2017; Siegal-Hawley, 2016). Local realtors showed white parents certain listings; homeowners kept their property in white hands (Massey & Denton, 1993; McGhee, 2021; Orfield, 2013; Rothstein, 2017). Town councils zoned for single-family homes only; apartment building permits, denied (Jackson, 1985; Massey, 2008; McGhee, 2021; Orfield, 2013; Rothstein, 2017; Siegal-Hawley, 2016). Passing on most public transit, they made themselves hard to get to (Jackson, 1985). Pricing people out, on purpose.

And when all of this worked, when suburbs boomed with white people and middle/upper class people—and typically these were the same people—towns needed to expand and schools needed to be built. School boards, councils, and voters decided where the boundaries would be, whom to count as a resident, whom to include in a school district. On the maps they drew, the district lines took twists and turns, holding white and affluent space inside (Baker et al., 2020; Baker et al., 2022; Knight et al., 2022; Massey, 2008; McGhee, 2021; Orfield, 2013; Owens, 2023; Owens & Rich, 2023; Ryan, 2010; Siegal-Hawley, 2016; Stroub & Richards, 2013). But like all borders, these weren't just lines on a map, these were procedures for controlling entry, and they effectively became "fences to separate the races," as Thurgood Marshall had warned (*Milliken v. Bradley*, 1974, p. 804). The wealth that school boards raised from sprawling homes and shopping malls was fenced off, too.

Today, there are suburbs that are more diverse, particularly the inner-rings, closer-in to cities (Lichter et al., 2023; Owens & Rich, 2023). Yet the boundary separating cities and suburbs continues to be a bright red line. This is especially true of the gulf in our metro areas between the outlying, farther-out suburbs, like the one being considered here, and the cities at their heart. The students who go to school in these places remain separated—by race and class, funding and educational opportunity (Baker et al., 2022; Knight et al., 2022; Lichter et al., 2023; Owens & Rich, 2023; Sosina & Weathers, 2019). We've moved forward in time, but "the urban-suburban divide remains an important stratifying force" (Owens & Rich, 2023, p. 26).

I think of this as history and power, working together. We have this history of how suburbs were created—how they became white and wealthier—but we also have the power that became concentrated there, which anchors the past in place and pushes back on change. The deeper thread of exclusion is still active.

❖

Creating New Realities

I'm saying all this because we tend to naturalize our present-day experience. To express where we live as a matter of choice or affordability or comfort. To characterize a school's quality as a matter of involved parenting, or the community's values, or the simple circumstance of limited funds. Without seeing the policies and history and exclusion that run underneath where we live and go to school.

At the start here, I'm trying to loosen your grip on reality, so you do not take the funding or the demographics of educational inequality as normal and done. So you picture, from this brief overview, disparity as in motion: it was started intentionally, and it is being maintained, mindfully and not. This comes from Paulo Freire, who's said if we can see how reality is being made—that there's flux even when powerful forces are tightening it down—we can imagine stepping in to make something different (Freire, 1998, 2006). Which brings up possibility. And hope.

Just like in Metro though, I'm not going to leave you with the disparity and expect you to climb out of it all by yourself. It's too steep. With the kids, we knew we needed to help them figure out what to do with their shock and sadness over their schools' dramatic differences. It was important to fit something positive to all that negative. The good came from the kids' side-by-side, city-and-suburb collaboration. The good came from experiencing action, knowing what making change feels like.

Having done this for a little while, I know you're going to need that too: some tactile feeling for the struggle, some model for creating new realities. You're going to need some shape to that hope. Luckily, I have something for you. It's called the Metropolitan Community Project.

❖

Notes

1. "Taylor" and "Wyndham" High are pseudonyms, in place to help protect the anonymity of the participants in the Metropolitan Community Project
2. The teachers in Metro ask the Metro students to refer to them as they would at school. In line with this request, the book uses the honorific of "Ms." or "Mr." combined with last-name pseudonyms for all Wyndham and Taylor teachers on the Metro facilitation team.
3. Please see the appendix for a directory of schools, students, teachers, organizers, and community-based organizations in the Metropolitan Community Project.
4. The community-based organizers in Metro have an informal rapport with the Metro students and ask to be referred to by their first names. In keeping with this tradition, the book provides them with first-name pseudonyms to protect their identities. But I've also added the honorific of "Ms." or "Mr." to communicate that they are equally-situated members of the Metro facilitation team, alongside their teacher counterparts.

References

Baker, B. (2018). *Educational inequality and school finance: Why money matters for America's students.* Cambridge, MA: Harvard University Press.

Baker, B., Di Carlo, M. & Green, P. (2022). *School segregation and school funding: How housing discrimination reproduces unequal opportunity.* Albert Shanker Institute.

Baker, B., Srikanth, A., Cotto, R. & Green, P. (2020). School funding disparities and the plight of Latinx children. *Education Policy Analysis Archives, 28*(135): 1–26.

Brown v. Board of Education of Topeka 347 U.S. 483 1954.

Candelaria, C. & Shores, K. (2019). Court ordered finance reforms in the adequacy era: Heterogeneous causal effects and sensitivity. *Education Finance and Policy, 14*(1): 31–60.

Darling-Hammond, L. (2013). Inequality and school resources: What it will take to close the opportunity gap. In P. Carter & K. Welner (Eds.), *Closing the opportunity gap: What America must do to give every child an even chance.* Oxford: Oxford University Press.

Farrie, D. & Sciarra, D. (2021). *Making the grade: How fair is school funding in your state?* Education Law Center.

Freire, P. (1998). *Pedagogy of freedom: Ethics, democracy, and civic courage.* Lanham, MD: Rowman & Littlefield.

Freire, P. (2006). *Pedagogy of the oppressed* (30th anniversary ed.). New York, NY: Continuum.

Hyman, J. (2017). Does money matter in the long run? Effects of school spending on educational attainment. *American Economic Journal: Economic Policy, 9*(4): 256–280.

Jackson, K. (1985). *Crabgrass frontier: The suburbanization of the United States.* Oxford: Oxford University Press.

Jackson, C. K. (2020). Does school spending matter? The new literature on an old question. In L. Tach et al. (Eds.), *Confronting inequality: How policies and practices shape children's opportunities.* American Psychological Association.

Jackson, C. K., Johnson, R. & Perisco, C. (2016). The effects of school spending on educational and economic outcomes: Evidence from school finance reforms. *The Quarterly Journal of Economics, 131*: 157–218.

Knight, D., Hassairi, N. & Martinez, D. (2022). Segregation and school funding disparities in California: Contemporary trends 50 years after *Serrano*. *BYU Law Journal, 1*(6): 1–29.

LaFortune, J., Rothstein, J. & Schazenbach, D. (2018). School finance reform and the distribution of student achievement. *American Economic Journal: Applied Economics, 10*(2): 1–26.

Lee, K.-G. & Polacheck, S. (2018). Do school budgets matter? The effect of budget referenda on student dropout rates. *Education Economics, 26*(2): 129–144.

Leone, H. (2020, December 3). Children from poorer Chicago areas are still less likely to attend top-performing high schools, despite CPS efforts to even the playing field, new report finds. *Chicago Tribune.*

Lichter, D., Thiede, B., & Brooks, M. (2023). Racial diversity and segregation: Comparing principal cities, inner-ring suburbs, outlying suburbs, and the suburban fringe. *RSF Journal of the Social Sciences, 9*(1): 26–51.

Llowen, J. (2018). *Sundown towns: The hidden dimension of American racism.* New York, NY: The New Press.

Massey, D. (2008). *Categorically unequal: The American stratification system.* New York, NY: Russell Sage.

Massey, D. & Denton, N. (1993). *American apartheid: Segregation and the making of the underclass.* Cambridge, MA: Harvard University Press.

McGhee, H. (2021). *The sum of us: What racism costs everyone and how we can prosper together.* New York: One World.

Milliken v. Bradley 418 U.S. 717 1974.

Oakes, J. & Rogers, J. (2006). *Learning power: Organizing for education and justice.* New York, NY: Teachers College Press.

Orfield, G. (2013). Housing segregation produces unequal schools: Causes and solutions. In P. Carter & K. Welner (Eds.), *Closing the opportunity gap: What America must do to give every child an even chance.* Oxford: Oxford University Press.

Owens, A. (2023). Separate and unequal: The need for nuanced accounting of the inequalities created by segregation. *Poverty and Race, 32*(2): 9–10.

Owens, A. & Rich, P. (2023). Little boxes all the same? Racial-ethnic segregation and educational inequality across the urban-suburban divide. *RSF Journal of Social Sciences.* 9(2): 26–54.

Reardon, S. & Owens, A. (2014). Sixty years after *Brown*: Trends and consequences of school segregation. *Annual Review of Sociology,* 40: 199–218.

Rich, P. & Owens, A. (2023). Neighborhood-school structures: A new approach to the joint study of social contexts. *Annual Review of Sociology,* 49: 297–317.

Rothstein, R. (2017). *The color of law: A forgotten history of how our government segregated America.* New York, NY: Liveright.

Roy, J. (2011). Impact of school finance reform on resource equalization and academic performance: Evidence from Michigan. *Education Finance and Policy, 6*(2): 137–167.

Ryan, J. (2010). *Five miles away, a world apart: One city, two schools, and the story of educational opportunity in modern America.* Oxford: Oxford University Press.

Siegal-Hawley, G. (2016). *When the fences come down: Twenty-first century lessons from metropolitan school desegregation.* Chapel Hill, NC: The University of North Carolina Press.

Sosina, V. & Weathers, E. (2019). Pathways to inequality: Between-district segregation and racial disparities in school district expenditures. *AERA Open, 5*(3): 1–15.

Stroub, K. & Richards, M. (2013). From resegregation to reintegration: Trends in the racial/ethnic segregation of metropolitan public schools, 1993–2009. *American Educational Research Journal, 50*(3): 497–531.

Warren, M. & Mapp, K. (2011). *A match on dry grass: Community organizing as a catalyst for school reform.* Oxford: Oxford University Press.

Lafortune, J., Rothstein, J., & Schanzenbach, D. (2018). School finance reform and the distribution of student achievement. *American Economic Journal: Applied Economics, 10*(2), 1–26.

Lee, K., & Polachek, S. (2018). Do school budgets matter? The effect of budget referenda on student dropout rates. *Education Economics, 26*(2), 129–144.

Leone, H. (2020, December 1). Children in [illegible] are still less likely to attend top-performing high schools despite CPS' [illegible] to even the playing field, new report finds. *Chicago Tribune*.

Lichter, D. T., Parisi, D., & Taquino, M. (2015). [illegible] Racial diversity and [illegible]: Comparing principal cities, [illegible] and the suburban fringe. *RSF: The Russell Sage Foundation Journal of the Social Sciences, 1*(1), [illegible].

Loewen, J. (2018). *Sundown towns: A hidden dimension of American racism*. New York, NY: The New Press.

Massey, D. (2008). *Categorically unequal: The American stratification system*. New York, NY: Russell Sage.

Massey, D., & Denton, N. (1993). *American apartheid: Segregation and the making of the underclass*. Cambridge, MA: Harvard University Press.

McGhee, H. (2021). *The sum of us: What racism costs everyone and how we can prosper together*. New York: One World.

Milliken v. Bradley, 418 U.S. 717 (1974).

Oakes, J., & Rogers, J. (2006). *Learning power: Organizing for education and justice*. New York, NY: Teachers College Press.

Orfield, G. (2013). Housing segregation produces unequal schools: Causes and solutions. In P. Carter & K. Welner (Eds.), *Closing the opportunity gap: What America must do to give every child an even chance*. Oxford: Oxford University Press.

Owens, A. (2020). [illegible] The need for [illegible] of the [illegible]. *Poverty and Race*, [illegible].

Owens, A., [illegible] (2016). Little boxes [illegible]: Racial/ethnic segregation and [illegible] in metropolitan [illegible]. *RSF: Journal of the Social Sciences*, [illegible].

Reardon, S., & Owens, A. (2014). 60 years after Brown: Trends and consequences of school segregation. *Annual Review of Sociology, 40*, 199–218.

[illegible] & Owens, A. (2023). Neighborhood–school structures: A new approach to the joint study of social contexts. *Annual Review of Sociology*, [illegible].

Rothstein, R. (2017). *The color of law: A forgotten history of how our government segregated America*. New York, NY: Liveright.

Roy, J. (2011). Impact of school finance reform on resource equalization and academic performance: Evidence from Michigan. *Education Finance and Policy, 6*(2), 137–167.

Rury, J. (2020). [illegible] *the city, the schools, and the story of* [illegible] *in modern America*. Oxford: Oxford University Press.

Siegel-Hawley, G. (2016). *When the fences come down: Twenty-first century lessons from metropolitan school desegregation*. Chapel Hill, NC: The University of North Carolina Press.

Sosina, V. E., & Weathers, E. S. (2019). Pathways to inequality: Between-district segregation and racial disparities in school district expenditures. *AERA Open, 5*(3), 1–15.

Stroub, K. J., & Richards, M. P. (2013). From resegregation to reintegration: Trends in the racial/ethnic segregation of metropolitan public schools, 1993–2009. *American Educational Research Journal, 50*(3), 497–531.

[illegible], M., & [illegible], S. (2019). [illegible] *for school reform*. Oxford: Oxford University Press.

CHAPTER TWO

School Resources Lost & Found

On Tour with the Wyndham Students: Taylor High, Chicago

WE'RE IN TAYLOR IN the hallway. It's mostly lockers and shiny floors, as expected. But on the wall facing us is a colorful mural of farmworkers in protest. Andy remarks proudly that the art "represents our culture," and she taps a depiction of César Chávez to illustrate.[1] Caroline, who's visiting from Wyndham, calls the mural "cool" and "really good." Seeing more around every corner, she exclaims, "The murals are everywhere!"

Once she's home in the suburbs, Caroline thinks, "All the murals on the walls—they have a lot more culture in their school" than she does in hers. As though, perhaps, something valuable might be missing where she's from.

The period's already begun, so we make our way to art. A teacher in an apron greets us, and Andy asks her to explain today's project. "They're building an armature," the teacher replies. She holds up a painted papier-mâché heart to give us an example of what the class is making. Earlier in the week, the students designed a shape and created a wire form. Now they are covering it with masking tape. We observe for a bit, making our way around the lab tables. About thirty students grapple with strips of tape and newsprint.

When we exit, Andy asks Caroline if she takes art. "Yes," she says, "but there are a lot of kids in that class," gesturing back to where we just came. "In my class, it's not close to that." She also learned on the tour that, at Taylor, "With art classes, they didn't offer that many. I think those are good escapes to have, which they don't really."

Back in the hallway, Andy points to the pennants hanging overhead, saying these are the colleges of Taylor alumni. Most of the flags depict in-state schools, but one is from the University of Michigan.

At Wyndham, Caroline remarks later, college is "on everyone's minds, but it's not displayed." She guesses this is because at her school, "everyone is expected to go to college, and they know they're going. But there," at Taylor, "it's not definite," so the flags help make it seem possible.

We go next to AP Biology. The teacher is reviewing the polymerase chain reaction, pausing at moments to let students fill in key facts. Today, he says, the class will do an electrophoresis simulation "on paper." Next week will be a DNA lab, "with little gels," to see the reaction up close. He asks the students to get out their reading, which is a photocopied packet from a textbook. We leave as they begin a review.

Outside, Shana asks if Taylor has "block schedules for science." The reason she's asking, she explains, is that lab-work lasts for two periods at Wyndham so they can do more in-depth experiments. That is not how it works at Taylor, Lena replies. "We only have one period for science." "And," Anna says, "it's really hard for us to do labs because we don't have the material." She only discovered her talent for science her senior year when she was finally able to investigate hands-on.

Maggie, who's from Wyndham, notices this need too, saying later, "In science lab, we have more advanced equipment than they do," at Taylor. "If you're not able to participate in experiments," she imagines, "it's hard to have a deeper understanding."

When we enter the cafeteria, kids look up from their lunches. They are sitting at collapsible brown tables, in a huge open space with linoleum floors, fluorescent lights, and the Taylor mascot painted on the walls. In a central aisle are large rubber trash cans for students to scrape their trays. To the right is the buffet line, with hot food in chafing dishes being served by women in hairnets. Anna shows us the new cash registers and the fruit "they make us take." She explains, "They do think about our health, they give us fruit every Tuesday. And for lunch, it's basically a chicken patty. That's what they give us."

Maggie asks if students have to pay, and Anna says, "No, we get free lunch, or reduced lunch, depending on the income of our parents."

Shana wants to know if students are allowed to go somewhere else once they get their food. Anna says yes, but only "if you have a legitimate reason to leave. If you need to do make-up work, you can go, but it depends on the security guards," who are posted at the entryways. If students can't get permission, or if the library is closed (which happens often because the librarian's only part-time), they are stuck doing work in the cafeteria. Concentration there is tough to come by, though. "When we have an assignment," Angelica says, "you can't get it done in the lunchroom because it's too noisy."

Shana thinks afterwards about how much more flexibility she has at Wyndham to decide where to eat, spend her free time, and complete her work, rather than being "confined to a certain classroom or cafeteria for every single period."

Touring the cafeteria at Taylor High. Photo courtesy of author.

It's down the stairs now and through a large metal door. Behind a black, chain-link metal fence are a few exercise machines and some stacked barbells. Lena says this is the school's weight room. So the Wyndham students understand, I ask, "And where are we?" "We're in the boys' locker room," Lena replies.

Amanda looks startled. "How do girls use it?" Lena answers, "Not a lot of girls join or use this. In P.E., the guys change, and then after five minutes, the teacher tells us to come in. At the end of class, we leave five minutes before so the boys can change back."

Lena adds that this facility wouldn't be here at all without community support. "The equipment was donated by a former student" who went on to become a professional athlete. "That's so great!" reacts Maggie.

The Taylor students are excited about the next part of the tour; many of them have never seen the pool even though they go here. An athletic coach leads us in. We stand on the deck staring into the water. The pool is "about 20 meters long," the coach says, but he wishes it "looked nicer" for the visitors. It's been "down for two years," he explains; the "heater went out" and something is wrong with the filter. "We're trying to start a swim team. It's a work in progress."

After the pool, we walk back upstairs to see band. The teacher interrupts the music so he can speak with the Wyndham students. "Do any of you play an instrument?" he asks. Shana raises her hand to say, "I play the violin." "And when did you start playing? Probably fourth or fifth grade, right?" Shana answers, "Second grade." The teacher responds, "That doesn't happen in Chicago," because music is a rarity until high school, and most families can't afford private lessons. "To give you an example, I have four periods of beginning band and only one period of advanced band." He turns back to his class to resume the song.

In play, the musicians seem motivated and practiced, except for a student plinking tentatively on the xylophone. When the piece is over, Maggie gives her praises, "You guys sound great!"

Amanda asks about the class's instruments. The teacher says he just received a grant and is excited to get some things on his wish list. The instruments, he explains, "get used a lot, five periods every day, for the past 10 to 12 years. Some of them are still playing well, but some of the saxophones, for example, are so awful they don't play. The clarinet and the trumpet are cheaper than the sax. So you have to make a choice: should I get two trumpets or one saxophone? I'm not sure if those kinds of decisions happen in the fine arts program at your school." The Wyndham students look down at their feet. Seeing this, the teacher adds, "Not that it's not a great school. I'm sure it is."

Getting ready to lead the class again, he says, "It's not easy but that's the way it's going to have to be. We work hard." We listen for a little while more, and when we turn to leave, the band students wave and thank us for coming.

It's between classes, and the passing period is filled with cheerful noise. Taylor students call out to friends down long hallways, meet each other at their lockers for quick chats, and give out hugs or complicated handshakes. For the umpteenth time today, someone greets Andy as we go by. Caroline asks her in a complimentary tone, "Do you know *everyone* in this school?" The sound of the security guards and the P.A. system urging kids to get to class just adds to the hubbub.

Later in the day, in a debrief, Jade remarks on the convivial scene: "A lot of the students were saying hi to each other." Jashaundra says she even saw someone "singing out loud" in the hallway. "Oh, that was Patricia," Trina says, as if being filled with song is just her natural state.

Moving slowly through the hallway busyness makes us a little late to language class. When we get there, small groupings of students are conferring about a worksheet, periodically referencing their open textbooks.

We gather around the teacher's desk. So as not to disturb the class, he quietly explains that we are in AP Spanish. Today, the students are working on grammar, and he is going through their homework. He points our attention to the masks hanging in the back of the room and says these are modeled on the artwork of an "indigenous group that lived mainly in the Caribbean. So we try to do culture."

The teacher asks the Wyndham students if they take Spanish. Maggie does, but Caroline takes Chinese and Brian takes Latin. Hearing this, the teacher says there used to be Latin at Taylor, but the teacher retired and was not replaced. At Taylor, "the language department is getting smaller and smaller." Caroline asks what languages are left, and the teacher replies, "Spanish and French."

"And French only goes up to French II," Andy interjects. That's true, says the teacher, and on top of that, levels I and II are offered only in alternate years. "Unfortunately, the budget constraints being what they are . . .," his voice trails off. "That's crazy," Caroline responds. The teacher agrees. He asks wishfully, "What are your language classes like? Do you have lots of fancy labs?"

Wyndham does have language labs, and Maggie later notes the discrepancy. "I didn't see any technology that could be used" during language instruction at Taylor, she says. "In the Spanish rooms" at Wyndham, "when we're recording how we're speaking, that's a major thing to how I learn Spanish."

In the hallways at Taylor High. Photo courtesy of author.

Down the hall, another language teacher is locking up. When she sees Andy, she lets us in, telling her she missed a "fun activity" today comparing two Mexican singers.

The room is strung with colorful paper cutouts that Andy's class made for Día de los Muertos. Something catches Caroline's eye, and Andy explains, "Us Mexicans, we do this. This is an altar we build when someone passes away. One person brings in food, another person brings in candles. And we eat a special kind of bread." She confers with Jerry, and adds, "I think it's called pan de muerto. It's only available once a year."

Caroline asks if this is AP Spanish too. Andy replies, "No, Spanish I." "But you already know Spanish," Caroline objects. With a smile, Andy responds, "I know, easy A, right?" "But isn't AP Spanish an easy A?" Caroline asks. "No," says Andy, "because I don't know a lot of the grammar and I can't read it very well."

What Andy doesn't say is that she started at Taylor learning French, but without a more advanced class to take this year, her counselor rerouted her to beginning Spanish.

Back in the hallway, Andy casually says something about the police office, which is staffed by the Chicago Police Department. Caroline sounds surprised. "You have a police station?" Andy says it's not quite a police station but there are police officers. Caroline asks if they can arrest students, and Andy replies, "Yeah, pretty much."

Next is the attendance office, where Andy states you go to get a "pass to class," for being late or absent. Tucked in the back is an area reserved for the parent mentors, a program supported by a community-based organization and small amounts of state funding.

The two mentors wave us over and ask Andy to translate from Spanish. Andy starts by saying, "It's their job to go to the child's house." Jerry corrects the translation: "student's." Andy amends the sentence and continues, "for people who are skipping school and have lots of absences. They get them back to school and then they have a conference at . . ." She asks a question in Spanish, and continues in English, "at the school."

Caroline asks, "Do you usually get the kids back in school?" The mentors reply, looking at Caroline, while Andy translates. "Yes. We find kids who are ditching and bring them back. We talk to the student, the student promises to keep going, then we keep checking to make sure they do. We make phone calls and also check on the computer to make sure they're going to class."

One of the women continues to talk, and Andy translates, "If the family needs food, we also help them out. Or if they're without a home." Caroline asks, "Does that happen?" "Yes." "A lot?" The women answer, "Sí." Through Andy, they explain, "If the parents are jobless, then the student doesn't feel like going to school." "Sad!" Caroline exclaims.

When the mentors say they work with around 20 missing students a day, Caroline looks shocked. "That many?" "Sí." "That's a lot of work," Caroline comments. The women agree. "We have to stay well-organized and we're here only four hours a day. We check on the students and make sure they're really coming."

Lena and Anna take us up to a place known a little ominously by its shorthand "Room 209." Lena explains, "This is the disciplinary office. If you talk back to a teacher, you get sent here. If you do something worse, you get sent downstairs to the other one."

We are about to move on, but Anna asks Lena, "Don't you think we should say something about our experiences with 209?" Lena shares, "Well, my experience is that during a passing period, I went to the bathroom," and when she got out, the bell had already rung. "We're supposed to have a pass, and I was asked for it, but I didn't have one. Basically, I was wrote up for cutting class. Even though I was in the bathroom, I couldn't get out of the problem." Anna affirms, "Uh huh, that's happened to me too."

Of the many differences Shana noticed after visiting Taylor, "The big thing is the lack of freedom. At Wyndham, we're supposed to have our IDs on us, but I go in the hallway during class, or go to the bathroom, and no one ever checks. We're allowed to go pretty much anywhere. And there, obviously, no one is allowed to be in the hallways."

A little while later, the Taylor tour guides take us to the other disciplinary office, the one for in-school suspensions. A uniformed security guard sits at the front of a converted classroom. There is a student in the back, listening to music through headphones.

Lena asks the security guard to explain his job. He speaks curtly, "I have a professional job as a babysitter. Except instead of pampers, I give out detentions." Shana asks what students normally get in trouble for. The security guard says, "It's usually minor infractions: if students are wearing a hat in the hallway, if there are electronic device infractions, if they talked back to a teacher. Whatever upsets the dean, they send them downstairs. Students also come here if they're late to class."

Lena asks, "What are your biggest challenges?" The security guard says, "I can't tell you because you're a student. If she was the only one here," he says, gesturing to me, "then I could tell her, but I can't tell you." Lena reacts. "I was just asking about the challenges of your job." He replies, "I know, but I can't tell you. All I can say is that we have a lot of disciplinary issues, and our hands are tied."

Amanda wants to know, "Is it ever just a misunderstanding that they end up in here?" The student in the back, who's actually been listening the whole time, shouts, "Yes!" The security guard yells back, "You shut up!"

To the question, he answers, "Sometimes yes. But the misunderstanding is usually because they got in trouble with the teachers, not from us."

The antagonism of the security guard strikes Maggie later as symbolic of "a major difference" in how Taylor treats school discipline. "There, they enforce one punishment for every student." But "when they give punishments here," at Wyndham, "they take the student into account and the situation they were put in," which seems fairer and more supportive to her.

The first thing we see when we enter the JROTC classroom is two students practicing how to lift, hold, and drop a rifle. The teacher, a sergeant dressed in a green Army uniform, approaches. His overview of the Junior Reserve Officers' Training Corps starts with a disclaimer. "We are absolutely not recruiters." He continues, "We are a leadership program that teaches life skills, to be successful when they leave out these doors." Caroline asks about the exercise continuing behind us, and the sergeant explains, "They're practicing their rifle drills."

There is a class in the back of the room, reading. Caroline asks the sergeant what they're learning. "They study the chain of command," he says. "No matter where you go, there is always a chain of command." In the program at Taylor, "All three instructors are retired Army. This is a partnership between the educational system and the Army. We are not allowed to recruit. Do I have access to recruiters? Yes."

The sergeant makes a point to stress JROTC's academic objectives. When students' performance falls under what's needed for college admission, "We push them," he says. "We spend time talking to them about their grades. If I have to sit there with Mom and Dad, or stomp on your chest a little bit, that's what I'll do. We do that because we feel we have a responsibility to make sure they get the education they need." The program also arranges for tutoring, he adds.

Caroline noticed afterwards "how prominent JROTC was" at Taylor, whereas at Wyndham, the armed forces are, in Shana's words, "non-existent." Both students left with positive impressions, seemingly convinced by the military-"tough love" combination described by the sergeant. Caroline mirrored his language in complimenting how JROTC "kept kids in line." Shana called it "a really good program" that was "kind of like our advisory program but more disciplined."

Learning about JROTC at Taylor High. Photo courtesy of author.

Lena knocks on a door and asks the woman who opens it if she's the nurse. She isn't, the nurse isn't on shift today. "But we share an office," the woman says. There isn't much room: half of the space is taken up by a plastic covered daybed. The rest holds a small cabinet with bandages and first aid supplies, a blood pressure gauge, and a desktop computer. It's hard to see how a nurse and a few ill students could fit in here too.

In a debrief of the day, Shana is taken aback. "People need nurses," she tells the Taylor students. "I thought it was a given. To not have a full-time nurse, I was surprised by that. And the nurse's office you do have, it's just an office with a bed to lie down in." At the end of the year she told me, "their nurse's office" was "one of the things that shocked me most" about Taylor.

We're running out of time, so we're not able to go to Anna's AP English class. But she wants us to know the teacher is "really great." A good example is what happened during the Shakespeare unit they just finished. "We're reading Macbeth. Have you ever read or heard of it?" Anna asks. Shana nods yes. "Well," the teacher "took all the students who wanted to go to the play" and used his own money for the tickets, Anna says. "He paid for the books and the shows." With funding so tight, field trips are few, and basic supplies are often scarce. Anna's English teacher, and many others here, try to personally fill in the gap.

This really registers for Amanda from Wyndham, who later recalls, "We heard that the teacher," at Taylor, "spent $500 out of his own pocket so students could go see a play of the book they were reading." What this shows is "the teacher really wants what's best for the students," and makes real sacrifices to make that happen.

Our last stop is Taylor's College and Career Center. When we get there, a staff-person introduces himself as the college counselor. "Only one?" Amanda asks. "How many students are in the entire school?" "In the entire school, there are about 850," he replies. "Oh," says Amanda. He adds, "I only started working here at the end of September," which is almost two months into the school year. "So right now, I'm focusing on working with seniors, and there are about 210 of them." He asks the Wyndham students how many counselors they have, and they estimate between six and eight. "And are those just for college?" he asks. Amanda says yes.

Shana inquires, "How does someone go about scheduling a meeting with you?" The counselor answers, "I don't schedule appointments with students. I just try to be available for students as much as I can. Students mostly come in during lunch or after school. That's usually the best one-on-one time, since throughout the day, I'm very busy." Shana nods.

I ask if he knows what the post-secondary enrollment rate is for Taylor. Last year, he shares, the rate was 40%, and the standard choice is community college in Chicago.

Maggie remembers Taylor's college counselor as "a great person, and he helps everyone, and he does as best he can. But I'm sure there's some things he can't do because he's outnumbered." She adds, "A lot of the kids at Taylor, at home, their parents didn't go to college, from what they were telling me. So they have no idea" how to apply. For her, at Wyndham, "it takes the pressure off to know: I have a college counselor and I'll figure it out. I have some security in that sense."

When the tour is over, Shana says: "Even though you can hear people talk about the inequities, it's more powerful to see it in person, and imagine myself going to school there."

❖

On Tour with the Taylor Students: Wyndham High, North Suburbs

We start, as before, in a hallway. We're at Wyndham. So far, it looks like any other high school. Waxed floors, lockers on each side, hand-drawn posters advertising school dances. Then Noa tells us we are going to the radio station. As we approach, our Wyndham guides shush us, pointing silently to the glowing "on-air" sign. We peer through the glassed-in booth to see students on mic debating a recent game; a sports program is in progress.

Next up is "gourmet class." At the classroom door, we're greeted by a teacher wearing a chef's jacket and clogs, her name embroidered on the pocket. Inside, 15 students sit at small tables, listening to another teacher, who is also in chef whites, explain a recipe. Like a time-lapsed food show, she holds up the finished product: a large chocolate bar layered with nuts and caramel.

On the counter are trays prepped with ingredients. When it's time to begin, the students grab their trays and head to their workstations, each outfitted with an oven-stove top, stainless steel counters, and red KitchenAid mixers. We watch as they get out pots and melt sugar until Abbey and Noa motion that we are moving on. Papi, who's visiting from Taylor, jokes, "You go ahead; I'll stay."

Passing through a school lounge, Lali asks Haley how many counselors there are at Wyndham, noting that at her school there are just one or two. Haley replies they have seven counselors "and that's just for post-high school counseling. We also have social workers, and your advisory chair is like a counselor."

I ask Haley to explain advisory, and she says it is a twenty-minute class first thing in the morning. The advisory teacher "takes care of everything you need at the school: if you need to switch classes, she'll get you the form; if you need to leave early, she'll get you signed out. Right now, we're choosing our classes for senior year, so we tell her the classes we want."

Lali says later, "They say they have, like, I don't know how many counselors or college guides. And right here," at Taylor, "we just have one. One for all the senior class. And, I mean, he didn't have the one-on-one talks and all that."

After a maze of hallways and stairs, we hover at the entrance to International Relations. The teacher waves us in, saying the topic this period is drones, and the class will eventually take a vote on their use. Groups of students are sitting at small round tables on colorful ergonomic chairs. He suggests that the Taylor students split up among the tables and participate in the discussion.

I sit with Lali and three male Wyndham students. A student asks her if she knows what a drone is. She shakes her head no. "We can show you a picture," he says, and holds up a black-and-white photo from his reading packet. He explains that drones are used to "kill people in Pakistan," and the targets "could be terrorists."

The student suggests they each go around and say whether drones are "wrong or right." One student says the drones kill "bad guys," but they can also kill "kids and wives. There's collateral damage and then people get angry, and then it's a whole mess." The first speaker asks Lali, "What do you think?" Lali answers, "I think you should not take somebody's life just because they're bad." There's a quiet pause, some breath-holding. A student breaks the silence to slightly agree, "Sometimes you're inspiring more terrorism." Another counters, "On the other side, you don't want to put Americans at risk."

The teacher eventually asks the whole class to come together. During the discussion, he types some main points on his laptop and the text is projected on a big screen. He asks someone to expand on a point he overheard in the small group discussion.

Back in the hallway, I ask Lali how she liked the class. and she responds, "Cool!" Haley explains International Relations is "one of the options" students can take for their history requirement. She asks the Taylor students if they have all of these "crazy different options," and they tell her they do not: there is only U.S. and World History.

At lunch, Lali is still talking about the class. "They were so into it! They were sitting in a circle. I liked that a lot. I liked that you got to talk about what you think in a small group. The teacher was there, and he knows what people said, so when he calls on you in front of the whole class, it's ok." Lali's friend Mia says she saw a "meaning of life presentation" in another class, exclaiming, "it was so awesome!" She adds, "I don't know if the Wyndham students even take advantage of all of the different classes. There's a lot."

An English class option called Literature and Film is already in session when we get there. About 20 students are arranged in a circle. The teacher, who's wearing a flannel shirt, glasses, and a short beard, is seated at a student desk with them. He gets us up to speed by saying the book they're currently reading is *The Road* by Cormac McCarthy, but right now, "We're discussing an unusual event that happened yesterday. Does someone want to explain?" A student in the circle answers, "Yesterday, we went to Wyndham Theater and saw *Godfather 1* and 2. And we ate pasta and cannoli." The teacher adds, "So it was six hours of watching the movie."

He asks someone to explain how the movie relates to the class's themes. A student dressed in a cheerleader's uniform raises her hand. Both Coppola, the *Godfather*'s director, and the class are concerned with "how the world shapes us and how we shape the world," she says. The teacher agrees. "This is an immigrant story. So some of the questions are: Did America do that to them? Or did they bring those values with them? These are some of the big questions we are asking."

For the rest of the discussion, there are always at least four or five hands raised, and just about everyone says something. The students explore the film's topic and themes and ask for clarification. As we're leaving, Papi comments, "They really participated in the questions."

Rounding a corner into what the Wyndham guides call "the music wing," we see a student playing an upright bass right in the middle of the hallway. The sound collides with a delicate classical piece wafting in from an open classroom door. We pause there, and when Matt receives a head-nod from the teacher, we go inside.

Arrayed in a semi-circle are the student musicians, holding brass instruments and consulting their sheet music; the teacher is standing at a podium with a conductor's baton. He stops the music periodically to give direction, and then they begin again.

Zoe whispers quietly to Bianca, "These people have been playing since like the fifth grade. They are really, really good." Bianca, who's visiting from Chicago, asks if Wyndham students have to buy their own instruments. Zoe answers, yes, but they can also rent, and community members often donate to the music program. This class is one of many musical outlets available at Wyndham, Zoe adds. There is also choir, orchestra, band, jazz, wind ensemble, and even opera.

The next period, we run into someone Zoe recognizes. "Weren't you in the music class we were just in?" she asks. He nods yes. "How long have you been playing?" "Since fifth grade." Zoe turns to our group, "I told you! Fifth grade!" The student adds, "But I'm not very good. I'm only second chair."

Even the name of the next place makes the eyes open wide: the "glass arts studio." The room is filled with natural light, and there are multiple worktables with clamps hanging off the edge. Bianca pauses in front of something radiating heat and flame, and a teacher explains that she's looking at a kiln that melts glass "to a bazillion degrees." Bianca replies, "Very interesting."

Further in, a student wearing safety goggles is cutting glass with an electric saw. At another table, we see students (also in safety gear) fusing shards of colored glass. The display cases outside the classroom show some of the finished work: beautifully decorated plates and glass animals.

In a debrief of the day, asked to comment on elective classes offered at Wyndham, and not at Taylor, Bianca says slowly, with humor and surprise in her voice, "Glass. Blowing."

Noa actually took glass arts last year. "I wish I could still take it now, but I can't fit it," she says. There isn't room anymore for a fun elective because her schedule is packed with classes meant to impress on college applications. Speaking of which, she shares, "I'm too stressed out," waiting to hear back about early admissions. "I'm checking my email every other minute." Meanwhile, "every other post from my friends is, 'I got into this college, I got into that college.'"

Learning about glass arts at Wyndham High. Photo courtesy of author.

The bell rings while we are walking, and suddenly students are all around us, rushing. We're swept up in the frantic pace, but traffic backs up in a narrow stairwell. Someone comes up behind Anna, who's a visitor in the school, and yells sharply, "Excuse me!" Anna, startled, frowns and moves aside. When we get up the stairs, our Wyndham tour guides pull us over. With our backs pressed against the lockers, we wait out the rest of the crush.

Papi tells me later that this part of the day shows a key school difference. "You know how in Taylor, the bell rings, and everybody talks in the hallway? Everybody's social. At Wyndham, it wasn't like that. Everybody was just quiet, walking to their spot right away."

When the coast is clear, we head to the library. Noa says this is a lunch period so it can get really crowded. Abbey points to an equipment room where students can check out TV news-style video cameras and sophisticated recording equipment. Noa shows us a carrel of textbooks. If a student forgets their book at home, she explains, these are available for checkout.

Nearby there's an insulated room packed with students hunched over books and laptops. "I live in this room every day," Noa says. It is the "silent study room," and she likes the "isolated seats" facing the wall but "spaces run out," so you have to get to them quickly.

Further into the library, there are open-plan classroom spaces with large tables, whiteboards, and projectors. Students can study there as long as a class hasn't reserved it. Otherwise, they like to study on the floor in the spaces between the stacks.

Noa demonstrates how to do a library search from one of the many computer terminals, and says, "You can also look up books that are in this library from home." "That's cool. There's a website where you can find books?" Papi asks. Abbey affirms this and says the librarians here are also "super-helpful, they help you with research."

On our way out, Noa casually notes that you can rent laptops from the library to use for the day. Papi asks how someone does that and Abbey jokes, "You use your ID as collateral."

In the debrief, Papi remarks on the contrast: "The library at Taylor, it's small and old. At Wyndham, it's big, and has lots of books. It's very resourceful. The Taylor library is fine; it helps. But Wyndham has a place where you can learn and it's quiet." In an interview he says, with a mischievous smile, "I'm going to steal that library."

Passing through the library at Wyndham High. Photo courtesy of author.

In the halls, in the middle of the class period, there are students everywhere. Lounging on the floor with their backs against the lockers, they are studying, snacking, and socializing. Taking in this sight, Papi asks if Wyndham students ever have to show their IDs to teachers or security. Noa pats down her pockets and discovers, "I don't have mine." Technically, Abbey says, you're "supposed to carry it at all times, but most people don't, and it doesn't matter."

Still inquiring about the freedom of movement allowed, Papi asks, "and do you have to be on time for lunch?" Abbey replies, "No, it's your free period," meaning there are no restrictions on where you can be in the building. Abbey has a hallway spot, and Noa, as she said, usually spends her lunch in the library. If you get a form "signed by your parents, you can also have off-campus lunch," she says. "You can't get in your car, but you can go off-campus."

Down yet another hallway, Abbey says she wants to show us the History Office. Inside are rows of teacher desks, piled with papers and decorated with tchotchkes and family photos. "Each department has its own office," Abbey explains. "This is where you come to visit a teacher," during a free period, or before or after school. Papi is very interested in this support system, and his questions elicit more detail from Abbey. "If you missed a day, you go see your teacher. If you are confused, you go in and ask a question. There is a room like this for every subject." Papi responds, "I would love to come to this school."

Trina is also impressed by this easy access. "What I noticed when I was there," at the suburban school, "were the offices: there was an office for English teachers, for Math teachers. The teachers are right there to help you." She continues, "Our teachers," at Taylor, "are helpful, but with so many less teachers, the teachers are busy," making it harder to receive their assistance.

We go downstairs to the nurse's office. To Trina, it looks like "a mini hospital": exam tables, cabinets filled with medical supplies, patient files, nurses wearing lab coats. A nurse tells us we can tour the main area but not the back rooms "to maintain students' privacy."

Trina asks how many nurses the school has, and the nurse replies, four. Trina tells her that at Taylor, "We only get one nurse, and she's only there three periods," two days a week. The nurse answers, "That's really different."

Noa gestures to the private areas in the back for "calling your parents" and "to rest." I ask if something I've heard at Wyndham is true, that students can take a nap in the nurse's office "even if they aren't ill." The nurse says, "We understand the pressures our students are under, and so sometimes we do allow that."

Trina told me later she was struck by how at Wyndham, "the nurses were on duty the whole school day and all school week." The nurse at Taylor, in contrast, "I swear, every time something happened to me, she was never there."

We go down to the basement to look at the gyms. In a huge open space, an indoor, spongy track encircles a weight room and exercise machines. Students with headphones move rhythmically on the ellipticals.

We watch for a bit, and then Noa takes us inside the "sports medicine center." There's a student with icepacks strapped to his biceps and another icing her leg on an exam table. A trainer works with a student pulling two handles attached to very large rubber bands. Still another student is balancing on a wobbly block.

A man wearing athletic shorts and a beanie cap comes up to us, and Noa asks if he can explain what they do in the facility. Their mission is to look after the health of student athletes, he says. "Like physical therapy?" Papi asks. "Exactly," the man replies. He adds that it's a "quiet day today because it's a game day, so we don't want to over-stress the students." When we leave, Papi comments, "I liked that. I didn't expect that."

Across the hall is a large, traditional basketball gym, with shellacked floors, arched ceilings, and bleachers. Papi says, "I can feel the energy already," and goes through the motions of doing a lay-up. I ask if he plays, and he says, "Yeah, we played yesterday. We lost though." Next-door is a more modern gym, with white walls and students playing volleyball. Deeper into the gym complex are two dance spaces. One is set up for a self-defense class and Abbey says yoga is also offered there. The other has hardwood floors and wall-sized mirrors, like a ballet studio. Three students spin and jump in a choreographed routine.

Haley knocks on a door and a teacher lets us into a room with a towering rock-climbing wall. There are about ten students sitting on the floor. The teacher explains this is an "adventure education" course, which fulfills the requirement for P.E. Their activities include rock-climbing, kayaking, skateboarding, and camping. Xavia exclaims, "Wow!" Lali says to me, as we walk out of the gym area, "They have so much stuff to do."

At the end of the year Lali remembers the athletic options at the suburban school fondly. "Their gym. Four tennis courts, and all that. That was fun. Their extra classes, their free periods. Like, I would love going there."

We stop at the door to the pool, and Shana flags a teacher to let us in. About twelve students in full SCUBA gear are bobbing in the water, while a teacher leads them through instructions on how to use the breathing apparatus. Shana explains that the water polo and swim teams also compete in this Olympic-sized pool.

Touring the cafeteria at Wyndham High. Photo courtesy of author.

We end up next to the cafeteria and Abbey suggests we go in. It's like the food court at a mall, with separate counters for different cuisines. Noa points to the deli buffet for build-your-own sandwiches. There are also tacos, smoothies, and stir fry made to order.

Papi studies the Wyndham students' trays as they go past. "He has a cheeseburger! There's pizza! Oh! There's pasta!" Trina exclaims to Papi, "You can bring your own lunch and microwave it! Wow! That's cool!"

Papi asks what the students are drinking. Noa tell us the Environmental Club raised money to install water bottle refilling stations in the cafeteria. We walk up to one and she demonstrates with a coffee cup she's been carrying around. She points to a ticker that keeps track of how many plastic bottles the school has saved.

To Trina, who goes to Taylor, these aren't small details. The food that "looks edible" and the "special water fountain" stay in her mind.

From the tour of Wyndham, "We basically have an example: like, why can't we have the same opportunity as this school right here?" The way Trina asks this is rhetorical, implying there is no valid answer, at least no reason that is moral and just. But to bring equal opportunity into being, Trina says, "We need people from both ends of the story to share what they feel."

❖

Note

1. The young persons' names in this book are pseudonyms self-created by the Taylor and Wyndham students.

PART II

Talking About Educational Inequality

INTRODUCTION

I'M WRITING THIS SECTION out of my surprise—at the students' lack of surprise. At least the absence of publicly expressed shock when the students saw each other's schools. How come there wasn't more, from the Taylor kids, of, "I can't believe you have this!" and "What?!" Why didn't the Wyndham kids say, as a Taylor teacher expected them to upon visiting for the first time, "This is your school?" And speaking of those Wyndham kids, when they were showing us around the radio station and the Olympic-sized pool, why wasn't there a little bit of, "We know this is kind of insane but it's also really cool"? Why did they seem more comfortable stressing what they saw as Wyndham's deficiencies—the age of the building, the intense competitiveness of the student body—than the supports and resources that did help? What was going on when the Taylor students, in planning their tours, talked about what not to show of their school?

Well, it turns out the divide did evoke surprise and shock, anger and fear. But these things were rarely expressed out loud when the city and suburban students were in the same room. Instead, on the tours, the visiting students often whispered to each other, or sidled up discreetly to their teachers or me, to share their reactions. Or they reacted more fully during separate debriefs, when only kids from their own school were there; and during their one-on-one interviews with me.

So this section is about how students talk to each other about inequality when they share the same spaces but radically different social positions. It's about where they get stuck, what they felt they couldn't say, and why. And, it's about the smaller moments, when the conversations turned open, and they shared more authentically how their school and life experiences diverged.

CHAPTER THREE

Communicating the Educational Divide: Wyndham

Presenting Wyndham: The Wyndham Students' Public Talk

LET'S GO BACK TO the school tours. After Haley takes the Taylor students to a class at Wyndham, she tells them it's just "standard English stuff." She suggests it would be "more fun if you just get to see the school rather than sit in classes. You get to see more and it's not as boring." She doesn't ask the Taylor students if they agree; she assumes they think so too. Moving on, Haley rushes through the library, pointing briefly to the "quiet study room" and the "project room." She flatly describes the multiple gym options at Wyndham: volleyball, floor-hockey, "lifetime sports" like bowling, yoga. To Haley, much of this is "standard stuff," and if there is something that feels special or rare, she doesn't say. It's all presented in the same matter-of-fact tone. On the few occasions when the Taylor visitors provide direct feedback, like when Lali notes there are two counselors to Wyndham's many, Haley doesn't react. She just continues with the tour.

The Wyndham students do pause to point out the school's problems. Simone tells her tour group, "Even though Wyndham has a lot of money, it doesn't look like it. A lot of the money is keeping the school in one piece." In the cafeteria, standing near the pasta, pizza, salad, and sandwich bars, Eve says the room is "super hot" and the roof leaks. Passing through the wing of the building that contains the architecture, robotics, and glass arts studios, Zoe tells us there is asbestos in the walls. Visually, Zoe says, her school is "not the most attractive building:" it "looks like a prison." The students from Taylor form a different impression. Just before Alex boards the bus for home, he looks up at the ornate towers and yells to his schoolmates, "This place is like Hogwarts!," the fancy castle in the *Harry Potter* movies. To the Wyndham students, the infrastructure is truly faulty. They joke about it with each other when they are alone. But they also, and this is important, feel it is necessary to highlight these deficiencies to their visitors.

Walking down a Wyndham hallway, Noa asks her tour group, "You noticed how no one is talking to each other in the hallways?" She wants the Taylor students to see. But just then, someone greets Abbey, exclaiming, "The math test was hard!"

During a whole-Metro debrief, in a Wyndham resource room, everyone is asked to think about what their school needs, and what difference it would make to have those needs fulfilled. How to answer this question when you go to a well-resourced suburban school?

The Wyndham students focus on their need for a friendlier environment. "I'm grateful for Wyndham and all of the opportunities it has," Claire says. "But if there was more community and loyalty, it would feel more supportive and less lonely." Wyndham has so much, but "a lot of people are not happy at our school," Noa agrees. Once, she got caught in the hallway crush and was accidentally kicked in the face. "Nobody said anything," Noa said, they just kept rushing to class.

The rushing, the isolation, the disconnection are byproducts of the intense pressure to measure up in a high-performing, status-conscious high school. "With the college counselors, we do get individual attention," Jade acknowledges. "But there's almost too much focus on college as the ultimate. It's like it's what we exist for: we are defined by college." The pressure comes from all sides: the school, peers, and parents. There is "so much stress to exceed all their standards," Kylie says. "So it's not just college" that matters, "it's a certain college and certain grades."

There is a "yes, but" quality to the Wyndham students' testimony, a way of saying, 'there are benefits to this suburban school, but there are also costs.' And the costs are real: the teachers, the nursing staff, the principal, and the students all highlight the acute stress, fatigue, and anxiety at this school, and the toll it takes on health and wellness. There is a companion inference, not meant to supersede these concerns and outcomes, but rather to consider alongside. In this same conversation, the Taylor students are describing a need for more college guidance, academic support, gym options, and technology—all of which Wyndham has in abundance. The Wyndham students recognize these resources, for the most part. But they also want to show, 'we have challenges and needs too.' It appears to feel more comfortable when everybody has problems, and everybody has strengths. Yet there's a canceling out that happens, an equivalency, that makes disparity harder to see.

The Wyndham students also talk about what their school gives them that they don't need. They make fun, in front of the Taylor students, of the school's seemingly frivolous amenities. "At Wyndham, they put all this money into football fields and iPads," Amanda says mockingly. "Like, they even want to have iPads for art. Are you kidding me? Like you need an iPad in art? That probably costs millions of dollars!" (An estimate that's pretty accurate, actually.) Amanda declares that re-seeding the lawn for outdoor sports is also wasteful. "The funding is so important but instead we spend it on football fields. Like what is that? Who cares?! It's just a bunch of grass."

This is funny, even a little refreshing. But Wyndham is not spending money on iPads and turf *instead* of more useful materials and supports. It's *in addition* to. And even these resources can matter to academics, and art, and athletics. This gets dropped, left unsaid. What is really happening here, I think, is that the Wyndham students are saying, 'We didn't ask for this,' and more importantly, 'We don't expect this.' As in, we are not entitled kids.

Presenting Wyndham: The Wyndham Students' Private Thoughts

Let's go behind the scenes. How did the Wyndham students actually feel, while taking the Taylor students on a tour of their school?

Well, remember Haley, who led her tour group in a no-nonsense, just-the-facts manner? Here's how she described what was happening on the inside: "It was *embarrassing* walking around and seeing so much that we have that we just don't need." She continued, "I felt like we were showing off. Like, we have a rock-climbing wall but they don't even have a nurse every day." It turns out that Haley's embarrassment, her feeling that she was "showing off" her school, was a common emotion. Caitlin felt that way too. "It's awkward to show them the giant nurse's office and going into one of our billion gyms. It was kind of uncomfortable to be like, 'So this is what we have.' Bragging is the only good way to describe it." I heard this view so much I started asking why. Maya explained, "We're almost bragging by showing them all of our resources and everything we get to use every day," when, "obviously, they don't have as many."

Seeing the sizable gap up close is in some ways the whole point of the Metropolitan Community Project. So why did leading the tour feel like boasting? If we take the dictionary definition, to talk with "excessive pride" or "self-satisfaction" about one's possessions, we can start to trace the Wyndham students' unease. In interviews, they repeatedly say they "don't deserve" the resources they receive any more than the Taylor students do, almost as if they are trying to correct the record. They are not proud of being on the advantaged side of extreme disparity, but they worry: by displaying their school so publicly, perhaps it looks like they are. "Maybe the way we were presenting it could be seen like that," Adrianna told me.

Filtering through the Wyndham students' responses seems to be a concern about what kind of people the Chicago students will assume them to be. "I hate how it probably looks like around here, sort of bratty and snobby, with the size of the houses and stuff like that," said Amanda. Jade, who felt "embarrassed" during the Wyndham school visit when "people from our school kept saying advantages," explained this was "embarrassment at being too privileged or sheltered." She added this emotion was widely shared. "I think a lot of people here feel they don't like the Wyndham reputation. Because some of it is associated with snobbishness or just really rich kids." Here, the Wyndham students translate the fact of educational advantage into judgment: snobby, bratty, arrogant, oblivious. They're afraid that their suburban school's abundance, and the wealth of their community, say something negative about their character.

While leading the tours, the Wyndham students felt a little bad about themselves, uncomfortable with how they might be perceived. They also felt bad about the Taylor students' reactions. "Honestly, I felt guilty most of the time," Jonas told me. "It came up when we were showing them around the school and talking to them about the different opportunities." Caitlin remembers Janelle's reaction when they walked together into a Wyndham gym. "She was like, 'Oh my god, I would kill to play volleyball here!' And I felt kind of guilty." Even the Taylor students' quiet prompted anxiety. "I felt a little weird because they were overwhelmed, they wouldn't say much, they were just looking and noticing," Claire said. For her, the tour was "uncomfortable at times, because compared to their school we have so much."

I got the sense from the Wyndham students that when they went about their business on a regular school day, they didn't feel guilty about the facilities or supplies available to them. In fact, many said the school felt pretty normal until the Taylor students came to visit. Annaliese "felt bad" seeing "the amount of astonishment to the things I didn't find astonishing." The climbing wall "made us seem off-the-charts cool," Jashaundra noted. But "when I think of it," she continued, changing her voice to an off-handed tone, "it's like, 'Oh, school.'" Claire commented, "We'd walk around," on the tour, "and I was reminding myself of all the opportunities we have." It was the presence of the Taylor students, and seeing the school through their eyes, that induced guilty feelings, by turning what felt natural into an example of injustice.

Metro students talking. Photo courtesy of author.

An unwanted feeling of arrogance, a sense of guilt, this is what the Wyndham students were going through when the Chicago students visited. A rush to neutralize these feelings could easily overwhelm a frank presentation of privilege.

And indeed, several Wyndham students spoke in interviews about how they consciously managed their discomfort on the school tours. For example, Jonas told me, "After talking to them about how different we were, I wanted to show them how similar we were. We went into the lunchroom so they could see we talk about fantasy football." When I asked him why this was important, he explained, "I wanted to show them we really are the same. Yes, we have more class opportunities, but we hang out with friends, we do the same things. Maybe there was a self-motive, so I could feel less guilty." Jonas embraced the idea that his job as a tour guide was to expose the opportunities available at his school. Yet the emotional work of talking about disparity was so taxing, he searched for a personal element that was the same.

When I asked Kylie what her goal was for the Wyndham tour, she replied, "To show them," the Taylor students, "how it's still just a high school. It's different but it's not that much different from theirs." She clarified, "I mean, our backgrounds may be different, but a school is still like a school. Even though there might be different resources within the school—a different atmosphere or a bigger school—it's still sort of similar." Kylie drew attention to the institutional sameness of high school to communicate what she and the Taylor students had in common.

Elizabeth was anxious to redeem the image possibly forming in the Taylor kids' minds. "I wanted to show them the parts that aren't bragging. Like the choir with special needs kids. Stuff that's good and helping people." Showing how her school helped people could perhaps reduce the impression that Wyndham kids reveled in their advantage.

An important point for Caitlin was to reveal what her school was lacking. She described how at Taylor, she saw kids hugging in the hallways, while at Wyndham, students looked straight ahead and rushed to class. "I wanted them to get the atmosphere more than seeing all the stuff. It seems like Wyndham has the upper-hand with school differences, but really we don't have the same sense of community." Caitlin genuinely sees Wyndham's competitive atmosphere as a flaw. But she also underlines it with intention to show that her school does not always have the "upper-hand."

There was an impulse to withhold from a full-scale tour as well, out of concern for the Taylor students' feelings. "I wanted to show them things, but I also didn't want to," Lisa said. "I didn't want them to feel sad or unfair." Maya also worried the tour was causing pain. "Near the end, I was like, 'We've got to stop showing them stuff. We're making them feel worse. They don't need to see everything; it's not that great.'" I don't think anyone from Wyndham literally short-circuited the tour. But the desire to protect the Taylor students contributed to their reticence.

What connects the Wyndham students' internal motivations is an inclination to close the gap. Emphasizing similarity, between schools or between students, is the most obvious way. But highlighting the school's problems, accentuating its contributions, or withdrawing from full disclosure are also ways of bringing the suburban school more in line with the urban one, by diminishing its abundance.

Even though she was a student at Wyndham and immersed in her environment, Laila had enough of an outsider view to act as a navigator, helping me see what was happening with her peers. "We go to a school where everything is provided for us, and then we go to these meetings with Taylor students, and they talk about all these things they don't have. I think it causes some Wyndham students to feel self-conscious in that context." She understood how reducing her school's upsides could help lessen the discomfort but believed this was ultimately misleading. "It's hard sitting next to a Taylor student and talking about how your school has these things. You also want to say something like, 'Well, Wyndham isn't perfect,' which it isn't, but a lot more things are provided, which is the truth." This was a difficult, uncomfortable truth, but Laila argued, "It's nothing to be self-conscious about. There's not really a need to dim it down. It's just to be aware that there is a difference. That's the whole point: there is a difference." That was the point, but she could tell it was difficult for her fellow students to let the difference between Taylor and Wyndham simply be there. The desire to "dim it down," to eliminate their guilty, show-offy sensations, was too strong.

Reacting To Taylor: The Wyndham Students' Public Talk

So now let's take a look at the suburban students while they're at Taylor. The communication discomforts extend here. About midway through the tour, as we walk down a hallway, Kenny asks Betty, "What do you think of our school so far?" "I like it," Betty replies. Kenny laughs and offers, "You don't have to; you don't have to lie." "No, I like it," Betty insists. "If I was lying, I would tell you." She laughs too, but it feels awkward.

In another group, as we're coming out of a classroom, Andy asks Caroline if she has any questions so far about Taylor. Caroline answers, "No. It's cool though."

Maggie is relentlessly upbeat throughout the tour. When she hears about the music program's shortages, she tells the band students they "sound great;" although the weight room is in the boys' locker room, it is "so great" that someone donated the equipment; and when a counselor explains how the school tries to overcome formidable barriers to college, she affirms, "it sounds like a great program!"

Other Wyndham students stay scrupulously neutral. For example, Jonathan sums up his time at Taylor, which included discussion of administrative turnover and the sometimes-inexplicable decisions of the current principal, with, "I learned there are many ways to run a school. There are so many ways and systems. It's interesting."

In other cases, the discovery of a limitation is absorbed without direct comment. Amanda asks if Taylor has a "language wing" like Wyndham, where there are "certain floors for certain classes." Anna tells her there isn't one, and anyway, Rusty adds, the French teacher just got laid off, so now, "we only have Spanish." "Oh, ok," Amanda responds. She reacts similarly when she hears there is only one college counselor for 850 students: "Oh." Jashaundra is shocked by this information, but she waits to express it to me, not her Taylor tour guides. Pulling me aside while we're waiting to see the pool, she says, "I can't imagine having only one person to talk to about college."

What is that old adage, 'Say something nice or don't say anything at all'? When they're together, the Wyndham students seem to feel obliged to say something positive about Taylor or say nothing. Or perhaps evenly observe that the schools vary, leaving out what those differences might mean. It's as if they think it's rude to publicly acknowledge disparity.

Which may explain why the military training program comes up a lot, in a good light. Addressing the Taylor students, Lisa says, "JROTC is a really cool program that I've never seen before." She's impressed by how it "helps you guys get better grades" and offers a "safe haven" within the school. The frequent mention of JROTC by the suburban students is curious, given that it's doubtful that they would ever enroll. Unconscious bias may be bubbling up in their belief that a military program is good for Latino youth. The enthusiasm of the sergeant in charge, as well as a few Taylor students, may have convinced. But my sense is that consciously what the Wyndham students are doing is looking around for an asset box to check and grasping at something that stands out from their school.

In the whole-group sessions, the shout-outs to the murals and the community-feel at Taylor carry a whiff of this too. It's not that these observations aren't sincere, but the comparisons are slightly overdrawn (Wyndham does have decorative art and socializing in the halls) and seem to fill a need for something good to say, when the Taylor students are there.

What's mostly left unsaid are the things that are difficult and hard at Taylor: the barriers students have to overcome, the resources they need but don't have. At least, not in front of the Taylor students.

Metro students talking. Photo courtesy of author.

When the Wyndham students do mention a difficulty, they are sure to accompany it with a strength. The first thing Jade says, when asked to comment on school differences, is something in the Chicago school's favor. "I like that things seem less isolated at Taylor." Only then does Jade mention the narrow focus on standardized testing at the school. Caroline does something similar. She notes the restricted weight room facilities and then says, "But at Taylor, there was a sense of community in the hallways." On the tour, when Maggie finds out there are very few support staff—just two counselors and a part-time social worker for the entire school—she accentuates the positive. "You probably have teachers who will talk to you?," she asks. Her tour guides both say yes.

The challenge-benefit pattern is particularly striking during one visit, when a panel of Taylor students describes the obstacles they face in getting to college. In the discussion that follows, rather than attending to these specifically, the Wyndham students focus on the upsides of adversity and the downsides of their affluent, college-obsessed school. "Some students at Wyndham think that money will save them in the end," Haley says, and expect a future "will be handed to them." At Taylor though, "it seems like all of the things they go through make people stronger," she observes. "It seems like that's the silver lining."

Limited resources, the suburban students seem to argue, build character and a sense of purpose, things that go missing in places awash in choice and money. "On the North Shore," where Wyndham is located, "there are a lot of opportunities that here at Taylor, you don't have," says Noa, which is definitely "unfair." However, "we have all these opportunities, but we don't know what to do with it." And without an internal compass, Amanda shares, many suburbanites blindly follow the path that's laid out for them, succumbing to the "pressure to go to college" when they "don't know what they want to do" with their lives. Unlike at Taylor, they imply, where college attendance requires singular vision and focus given the hurdles in the way.

How the suburban students talk about Taylor is a mirror image of how they talk about their own school: Wyndham has benefits, but it also has problems; Taylor faces challenges, but also has special gifts.

And of course, this is true: there is wonderful teaching and programming that happens at Taylor, as well as a more intimate feel and a celebration of culture. Struggling against very difficult circumstances, many Taylor students excel. Alongside this truth, it is interesting that the Wyndham students treat the barriers so gingerly and feel the need to publicly compliment the strengths. There's a balancing, 'on the one hand—on the other hand' quality, that makes the precise mix of assets and limitations at each school, and the size of the gap between them, more difficult to grasp.

Reacting To Taylor: The Wyndham Students' Private Thoughts

From interviews, we can see that the Wyndham students struggled with what they should say out loud about Taylor. "The most uncomfortable part" of Metro, Maya told me later, "was when we were at their school, and we were asked to compare their school to ours. We really didn't want to say anything."

> Maya: Their school, the outside is beautiful. But when you walk into a classroom, it's just lacking. When the teachers were questioning us, like, 'What do you notice?,' we just kept saying, 'our school is bigger than yours,' and that's about it.
>
> Me: What would you have said? What seemed 'lacking'?
>
> Maya: If I was being honest?

Interesting. When the Wyndham students talked about Taylor with the Taylor students, a few were willing to tell me, they held back. Jashaundra shared in our interview, "I wouldn't want to say some things that I said today in front of someone from Taylor." Everyone agreed to the ground-rule to "be honest," Claire noted, while doing a reflection in the Taylor library. "But I'd hear people on the bus ride home, and everyone would start saying things that they didn't say there." The Wyndham teacher who doubled as the bus driver noticed this, too.

What they declined to discuss—but saved for later, in interviews, on the bus, or with friends—were the essentials they noticed were missing from Taylor. Maya, for example, said if she'd been more "honest" she would've talked about the lack of projectors and computers in the classrooms, and the few books in the very small library. Jashaundra avoided talking about the scarce music and arts offerings, the solitary college counselor, and the minimal lab equipment at Taylor.

You wouldn't know they were thinking about resource gaps from the outside, because they were editing them out. "I felt uncomfortable talking about what Taylor doesn't have with people from Taylor," Elizabeth admitted. "You're trying to pick your words so carefully. If they have less than you, you don't want to bring that up." Jade promised she didn't even notice that Taylor had less until the students who went there pointed it out. "I'm not the most observant person of physical surroundings. So to me, it's just another school. I don't really notice. I didn't find anything shocking." Although she eventually listed the school's small size, a lack of computers, and "a lot less freedom," Jade insisted, "They talked about it—otherwise I probably wouldn't have noticed."

The key seemed to be that she, and many other Wyndham students, didn't want to admit shock. Instead, they substituted "stupid things that don't really matter" like, "you still have a pool," according to Maya, or said nothing at all.

Why are students "sometimes scared to be honest," as Claire put it? For her, it was "just something about how our schools are kind of different. So it's kind of uncomfortable to say, because it's not very nice." Again, it felt insulting to point out what the Taylor students didn't have. "I wouldn't want to make them feel bad. I don't want to be dissing on anyone," Jashaundra said. It didn't matter if that wasn't what she intended, Jashaundra told me. It still "sounds like dissing." She added, "I feel like other people" at Wyndham "feel that way too. That's why when you guys"—the adult facilitators of Metro—"ask questions at Taylor, the only people that want to talk are the Taylor students." Elizabeth explained her reserve with, "I just feel it would be really hard to be them, to be the ones with less things."

Talking about Taylor brings up the flipside again, the school with more things. "We have so much more" at Wyndham, Maya said. "And we didn't want to be like, 'We have this, we have this, we have this; You don't have this, you don't have this.'" Elizabeth made the sensible connection that, given how education is funded, sharing what her school provides above the rest is tantamount to admitting: "We make more money and have bigger houses." And this is "just not something we usually talk about," she said. "It's like a society thing. You don't want to talk about your money, how much money you make, or your wealth. It's a sensitive subject." True. Even teenagers know this is taboo.

That's not quite the core though. Ultimately, to the Wyndham students it felt like, in Metro, "We're always emphasizing the huge differences between us," Elizabeth said. Similarly, Amanda believed Metro involved "kind of comparing yourself to them." Comparing schools became the same as comparing people. And the Wyndham students took these comparisons personally, and worried the Taylor students would, too.

❖

CHAPTER FOUR

Communicating the Educational Divide: Taylor

WELCOMING GUESTS TO A low-income city school is much more vulnerable than hosting in a lavish suburban one. A tour means letting outsiders in on the struggles and hardships of the students who go there, and the possibility that these will be treated with the hardening of stereotypes rather than understanding. A tour also means visitors may miss how Taylor does help, and the effort Taylor students are making to succeed. To appreciate the discomforts in communication on the city school's end, we need to start behind the scenes, when the Taylor students are deciding what to show, and tell, their visitors.

Before Presenting Taylor: The Taylor Students' Private Thoughts

During a planning session, Taylor's Metro teacher asks what the suburban students should understand about the school. Alexandria replies, "They should know the good things we do instead of the bad." Moe hopes they'll see that, "We do the best we can do. It's not just all bad." Janelle wants the Wyndham students to know there are "kids at Taylor who are grateful" and "take advantage of the little opportunities we have."

There is a feeling of playing defense here, against the biases a suburban kid could bring with them, having absorbed what society tells them about city schools. The Taylor kids want to be sure the Wyndham students see "the good" inside the school, and inside the kids who go there.

To help the Taylor kids fulfill this desire, and to present a more complete picture of the school, Mr. Ryan begins a brainstorming session: "What are some positives in this building? Some of our strengths?" The kids answer: "a sense of school spirit," "the community work," the honors program, the school garden, the murals, how "everyone says hi" and "we give each other hugs and kisses." There are also "some really great teachers who help us in any way they can." They list off their favorite classes, highlighting the few electives—art, drama, leadership, psychology—and the available advanced courses. Also credited by the Taylor kids are the small set of clubs, sports, and after-school programs, tutoring on certain days in the library, and the availability of college counseling. Overall, Lucy wants the visitors to know, "it's a positive, good school."

In a broader sense, they want to humanize perceptions of kids who attend schools like Taylor. They are students who work hard, doing their best amid obstacles. The obstacles can be heavy, but Allie wants to share both "what we go through" and "how we deal with those problems," stressing the resiliency and added effort it takes to navigate an under-resourced school. Besides their own personal qualities, the Taylor kids want to honor the people around them. "They should know how we're supported, who stands behind us, who's there for us," Andy suggests. Theirs is a community of teachers, friends, and family helping them through school.

Mixed into the desire to emphasize the good is a fear of what may happen instead. What if, by revealing the school's challenges, the suburban kids end up thinking it's "just all bad"? Even worse, what if they end up thinking that about the Taylor kids?

With this worry in mind, there are topics the Taylor kids feel safer avoiding. Mario, for example, is assigned by his teachers to research Taylor's demographics for an overview they will give about their school. Searching on the district website, he also finds a summary of the school's academic performance. During a practice run-through, he states, "Taylor is on probation level three;" a label the school district uses for results on a state test. In a feedback session afterwards, several Taylor students urge him to cut this part of the presentation. Lucy argues, "They said we were on probation. I don't think we should mention that. It makes us look really bad." It is removed from the final version.

There are other things to steer clear of. Ailany asks, "What are we going to feed them? The school pizza?" Other Taylor students chime in: "that's nasty," "not the school pizza," and, "our lunch is the worst." Anna doesn't think the cafeteria should be on the tour at all.

Anna also wants the Taylor students to be selective about what classes to show. "We should choose a really interesting classroom," she tells her group. Trina and Slim debate which Band class to tour with the visitors, since some "weren't as good." In the morning, "I can hear them," Trina says, shaking her head in disappointment. Slim suggests putting Advanced Band on the tour list just to be safe. The students have trouble thinking of "a good class" to visit for Math because several are staffed with long-term substitutes. Papi argues to strike a class from the tour because of its reputation for unruliness.

The Taylor students worry that academic struggle, unpalatable food, and less-favored classes will be painted with a broad brush of negativity. It seems simpler to just take these things out of the tour.

As we'll see, these overlapping goals—to communicate strength and to curtail negative thinking—combine in sometimes confusing ways. The Taylor kids organize their school tour under categories like "the strengths and challenges of our school" and "the positives and negatives," which can give the impression that these equal each other out.

Presenting Taylor: The Taylor Students' Public Thoughts

During the tour, we can see the Taylor students emphasizing their school's bright spots. Out in the hallways, Anna pauses in front of a large mural, proudly stating it was painted by students, and she previews the coming attractions with, "there are murals everywhere in our school." She takes us up to her art class, where there are more paintings, this time mounted on poster board and leaning against the walls around the room. She tells her Wyndham tour group that "these were displayed just for you guys." "We knew you were coming," the art teacher confirms.

Downstairs, Angelica shares information about the academically-selective honors program that "helps students go to college." There's "a tutor to help you with your subjects" and "once a week, you go to the college resource center." She's been in this helpful program since her freshman year.

In a debrief with the suburban students, the Taylor students stress their most valued asset: the "friendship connection between Taylor students and teachers." Classes feel "comfortable" because their teachers are "helpful, almost playful" and "students and teachers can joke around with each other," says Mia.

They tell the Wyndham students that the suburban high school feels too formal and anonymous. When she was there, Ailany noticed, "the teachers didn't recognize their own students," sometimes asking the Wyndham tour guides if they too were visiting. Wyndham classes appeared "calm," but there's "not that much relating," Janelle said.

With the Wyndham students present, the Taylor kids say they prefer how students relate to each other at their school. To Rusty, Wyndham is a "cold shoulder" environment, where you're liable to "see new faces every day." She likes it better at her school where students "all know each other." Taylor students are "loud, rowdy, nice, and more friendly," Janelle vouches, intending all four descriptors as accolades. In the relationship-department, the Taylor kids assert, it is they who are better off.

The art, the programs, and the school bonds are significant to the Taylor students and help to buffer them from the harm of scarce resources. We can also see it's important to them to publicly claim their strengths, so the suburban students will not assume otherwise.

And, in meeting this need, the emphasis on assets sometimes tips into minimizing challenges. Leading her school tour group, Katie emphasizes the advanced band is "rated superior," but does not cover the music program's struggles with providing enough instruments. She points out a lab with the "newest computers" that "work really well," but again, does not describe how scarce a resource this is.

Opening the door to the gym, Katie takes a look, backs up quickly, and closes it again. "There's a sub," she says, in a nervous tone of voice. Substitute teachers are not uncommon at Taylor because of teaching shortages and layoffs. Katie's tour guide partner suggests we go in anyway. Students are lounging on the bleachers, while the substitute sits in a chair reading a magazine. Katie did not want the visitors to see this scene.

When Laila asks Moe how Taylor students receive college information, he says there is counseling help available to "take you through all that" and students use this resource "all the time." In his description, Taylor seems just as college-supportive as Wyndham. Yet Moe's perspective comes from participating in an honors program for high-achievers and is not a universal experience. With one college counselor for over 800 kids, most students do not have someone to personally take them through the college process.

In a later year, the college counselor, too, is laid off. The counseling room is still there, and inside, a part-time representative of a federally-funded college program explains his role. But the program's capacity is small, and only a handful of students are accepted. For the rest of the student body, there is no college guidance at all. Neither the Taylor tour guide nor the representative mentions this.

Of all the things to avoid, this one was the most important: there was no way, according to the Taylor kids, that we were going to feed the visitors the school lunch or make them sit in the cafeteria. They made this clear: for the tour, the regular, "nasty" lunch was out of bounds. So the adult facilitators got some money together for a catered meal, cooked by local restaurants and even once, a school mom. In the school library, on the day of the tour, the Taylor kids dole out gentle instructions on how to eat tamales (don't eat the corn husk!) and explain pigeon peas and tostones for their suburban guests. Instead of being uncomfortable, the lunch is a position of strength from which to teach less culturally literate peers.

When the Taylor students do bring attention to obstacles, they often pair these with a support. During a presentation to the suburban students about her school, Celia says, "One of the challenges is resources. We don't have enough books or supplies. One of the successes is the clubs and the tutoring." In another example, Janelle admits, "we're limited in counselors" at her school, "but the teachers are open to help." The format of presenting strengths and challenges like this offers a more holistic picture of the school and gives credit to teachers working way beyond their official job descriptions. But a casual listener may assume that the resources Taylor does have compensate for the resources that it doesn't, which is not the case.

The comparisons to the suburban school often work the same way and create even more confusion. In a debrief with the suburban students, Elani says Wyndham has "more art classes, but here," at Taylor, "it's smaller and the teachers really care." In the same conversation, Ailany says something similar about a different resource. "There are more language classes there," in the suburbs, "but we have ROTC, and they don't. We are all learning something."

These statements by the Taylor students are accurate: they are right to recognize the effort their school makes to provide them with an education.

But the Taylor students are entitled to the things the suburban school has—the language and art classes—*and* what they have; it shouldn't be either-or. And, in the bigger picture, the suburban school has way more advantages, and the city school has way more challenges. The stylistic convention of matching needs with assets is a well-meaning corrective to deficit thinking. But it can obscure this larger truth.

Metro students talking. Photo courtesy of author.

There are times when the obstacles slip through, when the Taylor kids lose control of the narrative. They aren't the only ones talking on the tour. The security guard says he's a "babysitter," and disparages students; the college counselor says he can't meet one-on-one; the band teacher calls attention to the used, squeaky instruments. At the cafeteria door, it takes forever to get through the line for scanning IDs, and inside, a student and a security guard start shouting. The P.E. class with the sub isn't doing anything. All of this runs counter to the message the Taylor students are trying to convey, possibly creating the wrong impression, perhaps reinforcing thought structures already in the suburban students' heads.

Which is why Corey feels the need to say out loud to the Wyndham students what they've been worried about all along: "Our school isn't that bad.

It's like every other school." But the second part is not right: the Chicago school is not like the suburban school, not really. And while the Taylor kids use words like "good" and "bad," this is not about judgment of any kind. It's about inequality, concrete disparity, and its very real effects.

After Presenting Taylor: The Taylor Students' Private Thoughts

On the tour, when the Taylor students narrated their school's assets, you could hear the pride in their voices. And indeed, they told me privately that this was their intention. "I wanted to show off what our school has, and it's not all bad like people think Taylor is like," Angelica said. "I was glad to show them the college resource room" and the honors program, she added. Similarly, Lali told me, "I think I did show off my school. I'm not going to say I'm not proud that I'm going to graduate from this school, because I am proud. I really like this school."

It's interesting how different this is from the Wyndham students, who were trying to avoid "showing off" or sounding prideful. The Taylor students know they're starting from a different place in public perception: instead of made-for-TV perfection, they believe people generally picture the worst when it comes to a neighborhood school in a low-income, urban community. So they take on the almost heartbreaking job of trying to counteract this image. Rather than a "boast" over excess and wealth, this task seems more like a shoring up, a way to stress talent and strength, and defend their school's dignity.

Lena certainly felt this responsibility. "I wanted them to know that I don't consider this school bad. I wanted to let them know this school can do so much things." She was happy this was communicated successfully. On the tour she led, "They did get the point. I didn't have to tell them this is a great school. As soon as they saw it, they liked it: how close it was, how people interact in the hallways." During the suburban kids' visit, Angelica told me, "I think they got to know a little bit more about what's inside of Taylor, and what they offer. There's people who actually want to learn and there's resources that can help us."

This pride is really important: to honor the students and staff who go there, to recognize the cultural expression that enlivens the environment, to acknowledge the inclusive atmosphere, and to credit the supports that are available. Celebrating the good offers hope and a sense of purpose to city high school students trying so hard to succeed in an often-difficult environment. It is important for the suburban students, as well, to ensure that stereotypes don't consume their understanding.

The Taylor students' pride swelled upon hearing the suburban kids' public reactions to their school. "They were really into the pictures on the walls," meaning the murals, recalled Trina. A Wyndham student in Maria's group "said the lockers were smaller at her school." Rusty related how "my group was really into ROTC. It seemed like they kind of wanted it." They didn't have cultural artifacts like "the masks hanging on the walls" in Spanish class, Andy reported. Elani heard the Wyndham students say, "the library was so organized and had so many books."

The suburban kids' highest admiration was reserved for the community atmosphere at Taylor. "They said it was more open and loose here, you can find your friends in the hallways," Papi reported. Janelle heard this as well: "They have a thousand students per grade level, so here they really did interact. They thought it was friendly."

Overall, from what Rusty heard, "they liked it" at Taylor. "They felt welcome." The suburban students came away with "a good feeling about the school," Maria said.

Without minimizing the need to recognize strengths, we can simultaneously consider an additional dynamic: that the Taylor students seem gratified, even complimented, when the Wyndham students "like" their school. Before, we considered how the Wyndham students felt the need to say something positive to the Taylor students about their education. Here, we see it is important to the Taylor students that the suburban students' reactions are positive. It becomes difficult in this context, when there are mutual intentions to validate and affirm, to talk about the very real limitations placed on this school.

Wanting the suburban students to like their school made the times when the message got away from them sting. In a Taylor-only debrief, after their visitors had left, Mr. Ryan asked, "What could've gone better?" Trina regretted that, on her tour, the suburban students witnessed a verbal altercation in the cafeteria. "If we had kept walking, they wouldn't have had to experience it." Janelle agreed, saying, "I would've preferred not to have shown them the lunchroom. They thought it was the craziest part of the school."

What else could've gone better? "Not going to the discipline office," Ailany replied. The security guard was too "harsh," she recalled, bragging about how, "I suspend them; they don't mess with me." These "cases are the extreme," Janelle objected. "There's a group but not the whole school," Jerry confirmed. They want to be sure the Wyndham students understood this too. "We told them," Lena said. "We told them not everyone is like this in our school." The Taylor students feel this pressure to protect themselves against negative generalizations. "I didn't want them to perceive the school that way," Anna said. "I didn't want them to perceive everyone that way."

There is a deep fear being expressed here: "Don't think badly about my school, please." And perhaps more centrally, "don't think badly about us." And from this fear, they wished they could've managed impressions a little more. In the future, Anna said, "We should speak to the teachers and staff ahead of time and tell them to talk positive rather than focusing just on what's wrong. Not everything is wrong at Taylor. Don't put things in these kids' minds."

This is hard: not everything *is* wrong at Taylor, but there are some things wrong. And the pressure to "talk positive" may gloss over some of these real challenges.

At Taylor, I also had a few navigators, students who could tell me what was happening with the communication styles of their peers. "There's pride, there's also pride," Slim told me, about the city students' avoidance of certain places and topics. "They don't want to be the worst." She explained, "It is kind of embarrassing that you see what they got," at Wyndham, "and then you show them what you got, and it's obvious that they have it better." It seemed natural in this situation to soften the obstacles and emphasize the strengths. "I would get what they were saying," said Slim, of her Taylor friends, "and I would feel that way sometimes." Even she wished she could've "avoided" the lunchroom and less interesting classes. "But I'll still be honest," she continued, "because it needs to get fixed, and people need to know what's the problem." For other Taylor students, however, the need to guard against outsiders' worst stereotypes superseded a more complete presentation. Given the power of these negative images, it was difficult to let both truths coexist: that their high school is worthy of respect and it has inequities that should be fixed.

The navigators, more comfortable with this duality, told me they didn't really need the Wyndham students' compliments. In fact, behind the praise they could see the stumbling blocks of communicating about disparity. "Some of their comments were really positive," Jaime said, "but at the same time, they were, for my opinion, just doing it to be nice. They don't want to be seen as all judgmental." Slim observed the same dynamic among the suburban students. "They still need to be more truthful with us," she said. "But that's hard. If I was in their position, I wouldn't want to be, because you feel like you're judging, or you might hurt someone." Katie supposed the suburban students held back because "they don't want to hurt our feelings. I guess they want to be nice about it."

The empathy here is pretty extraordinary: city kids from an under-resourced school trying to understand what it's like to be in the place of an advantaged, suburban student. And they intuited the bind the suburban students felt they were in, that being direct about educational disparity, particularly when it comes to insufficiency, sounds like judgment.

Yet while these Taylor students acknowledged the trickiness of the conversation, they believed it was necessary for the Wyndham students to be more forthcoming. Katie told me,

> We know Taylor isn't the best school. It needs more help, and it needs more funding. And when they came, and they said, "Oh, this place is great," it made us feel like, "Well, you guys go to school in like a mansion, like a castle. When you come here and say it's ok, it's not really ok." So I mean, being truthfully honest in their comments about the school—it might hurt us—but this is reality.

This reality was really important to uncover, Katie said, even if it was uncomfortable. In her ideal conversation, the suburban students would actually be able to say, "Your school needs help on this; you need more this." If they did that, Katie believed, "it would just bring more awareness to the fact that our school does need help. If other people are seeing this, that means it's real. It's not going to be hidden under something."

It sounds a little self-help-like, but here's what these Taylor students are saying: We need to recognize the problem before it can be fixed. And it's not just the Chicago students who can do this, but the suburban students as well. "Both sides need to be more honest," Slim says. In fact, they're arguing it's helpful when students from entirely different places and schools do this together. It's a different, harder kind of affirmation than saying "your school is great," but it's an affirmation, nonetheless. It validates the struggles Taylor students go through, making them "real," and lays the groundwork for collaboration. Holding back or papering over conceals the extent and the urgency of disparity. Talking clearly about the gap is a starting point for sharing the work to close it.

We'll come back to the language that the city and suburban students use about their communication though: by making "honesty" the principle they fall short of, they're a little too hard on each other, given the goodness of their intentions, and a little too personal about what is at its root, a political problem.

Working on a dream school. Photo courtesy of author.

Reacting To Wyndham: The Taylor Students' Public Talk

Whenever I explain Metro to someone, one of the first things they ask me is, "are the Chicago students shocked?" And, "are they upset?" The answer is only a qualified yes, because if you walk alongside them during the Wyndham tour, you won't necessarily know. There are some outgoing students who ask a lot of questions and react loudly when they see something different and new. Papi, for example, regularly exclaims, "Wow!" and "Cool!" and even a couple of times, "I would love to come to this school." Most of the audible, visible reactions from the Taylor students are like this—a surprised enthusiasm, not sadness or anger.

But for the most part, from what the teachers and I observe, the Taylor students tend to recede into the background when they are at the suburban school. In the arts and engineering wing, Allie and Anna walk the hallway as a pair, talking quietly to each other about what they are seeing. In the cafeteria, they point at the different food lines, and whisper, wide-eyed. Anna approaches me, and not her Wyndham tour guide, to say, "They complain their lunch is bad. But our lunch at Taylor . . ." Her voice trails off and she shakes her head. In the library, I overhear Allie and Anna discreetly noting the number of books and a difference in the librarian's demeanor. Watching a class practice intricate dance moves that involve long wooden poles, Allie says to herself, in a low voice, "We should have a dance class." The tour lasts two class periods, and by the second, the Taylor students in the group sit down whenever they can, rather than explore another gym or classroom. Sitting in student desks or on the bleachers, they stare into space or at their phones. Anna tells me she is tired.

In another group, Xavia and Lali walk together, listening silently to Haley's narration. There are no reactions or expressions of surprise. They have definite opinions about what they are seeing but they wait to share them until they see their Taylor friends or me. They don't respond when Haley says the English class is "standard stuff," but when I ask Xavia a few minutes later, she says the students in the class were "really engaged." Exiting the volleyball gym, Lali comes up to me privately and remarks, "They have so much stuff to do." At lunch, she excitedly tells her friends about the drone discussion she'd had in the International Relations class. Jaime is a little different, asking a few questions, including one about school security. Haley answers, "We have parapros, which is kind of similar." It's not at all similar to having Chicago Police in your school, but Jaime doesn't say anything.

The Taylor teacher, Mr. Ryan, noticed, "within the school tours, the Taylor kids would be towards the back." Mostly, they were silent, and "I would be the one asking questions," he said. Part of this had to do with the suburban students, who often didn't ask for questions or reactions. But he also believed the "Taylor students withdrew," and as a result of this mutual dynamic, "I didn't hear a lot of dialogue or discourse" during the tours.

A Wyndham teacher also remarked on a tendency toward "a very quiet Taylor group" when they were at his school but noted that his students could be "insular" in ways that diminished the back-and-forth.

What we're left with in this reticence, in this sharing of views with primarily same-school peers, are some missed opportunities for conversation. It's crazily obvious to the Taylor students that they don't have what the Wyndham students have. When they are uncomfortable saying so, when they can't talk about missing things they need, when they suppress their surprise over never-imagined resources, the size and the meaning of the gap stays obscured—for everyone. This is not to blame the Taylor students, but to think about why they may have held back and what contexts could have supported their fuller expression.

Reacting To Wyndham: The Taylor Students' Private Thoughts

So they were shocked. Wyndham upended what the Taylor students thought a high school could be. "That high school looked like it was out of a TV show," said Andy. "You go over there," Xavia said, "and it looked like a mansion. I never knew schools like that existed." Mia didn't either. "I'm shocked by everything they have. I never knew of anything like that." The contrast far exceeded Anna's expectations. "I never thought it was *that* much of a difference. It shocked me how big a difference it was." "I knew already," Kaycey claimed. But then she added, "kind of, sort of." Because, "to actually go and investigate, you actually feel the difference. It was surprising that it's this much of a money difference between the two schools."

Knowing there was this degree of shock and surprise, we can go back to the school tours. Xavia was one of the students who said little while she was walking Wyndham's hallways. She told me she was shy, so this was part of it. But she also said, when she saw "the electives that they had, the gym equipment—everything they have—that overwhelmed me. I don't think there's any way to prepare." This feeling of being completely overwhelmed, of seeing a high school that seemed unreal, like it belonged on TV, can help explain the minimal conversations with the Wyndham tour guides. It was, in a way, a stunned silence.

During their time at Wyndham, the Taylor students revealed they did have a running conversation going—but it was in their heads. When she was walking around, Lena noticed, "Their technology is way higher than us. I was like, 'We need something like this in our school.'" Of Wyndham students' flex time, Maria thought to herself, "the free periods? I'm like, 'Oh my god, I need one of those.'" Lali appreciated how the suburban students could take "dance as a class, not as an after-school, which I thought was really cool." She thought this—but didn't say it out loud to her tour guides.

It's a simple, natural response: we want some of the things you have, you have some of the things we need. Indeed, there were times when the Taylor students were able to say these things, and like we saw earlier, the Wyndham students felt guilty hearing them. But most of the time, this reaction went unarticulated until the Taylor students were safely back with their friends and teachers or in interviews with me.

A clue for their reserve can be found in how a few of the Taylor students framed their perceptions of Wyndham. "I'm not trying to be mean," Maria said, remembering the bus ride through the suburban neighborhood. "But the houses kept on growing by the street. They just got bigger and bigger and bigger." A question: why is this observation mean? Another scenario: Lucy states, "The Wyndham students have so much," both at home and at school. But she's quick to add: "It's not even about being greedy or because I'm hating." Again, why is a straight-ahead statement on the benefits of wealth greedy or mean?

Two other Taylor students went even further, characterizing their educational wants and needs as "envy." Anna said she was "envious" of the Wyndham students because "I feel like they were more prepared" for college. Andy told me, "I envy them for the resources they have." When I asked her to say more about this feeling, she replied, "I do envy it because I wish I went to a school like that."

This word choice sits uneasily because the teachers, students, and organizers in Metro all share Andy's wish: for every Chicago student to attend a well-resourced school. The whole point of the Metropolitan Community Project is to try, in a small way, to generate the relationships and actions that can turn this vision into a reality. It is not "envy" to desire a high-opportunity education.

But if this is the language the Taylor students reach for when they wish for suburban-style school resources, you can see why they would want to avoid it. Envy is "resentful longing," a feeling of bitterness towards someone who has more than you. It is one of the seven deadly sins, and in general, you're not supposed to feel this way, or if you do, you certainly shouldn't express it. It's mean and covetous towards others, and unappreciative of one's own gifts.

And so, the Taylor students offer assurances that they are not begrudging their partners in the suburbs. "It's a really beautiful school," Lucy says of Wyndham, "and some students get to have that school. That's good." No one is suggesting, she seems to say, that it's wrong to enjoy such a school. The intention is not to be "greedy" or "mean." From her school library in Chicago, Trina defends the Wyndham students against possible appearances. "They just were fortunate enough to be able to go to a quality school like that. Before people go off and just start judging them and blaming them for everything that's wrong over here, it's not their fault." It's sort of cute and lovely, this effort to protect very advantaged students from judgment and harm. And yet, by framing their reactions to Wyndham as "envy," they may not share these thoughts, to avoid sounding resentful and blaming, to minimize offense.

The underside of envy is ungratefulness, a character trait the Taylor students are also at pains to reject. "I'm not selfish when it comes to my school," Anna tells me, after admitting she felt envy. "I just wish we were able to receive better." Gratitude, she goes on, is the antidote to that wish. "I appreciate everything I have now. Of course, everybody is going to want more," she says, as though the impulse is excessive. Giving an imaginary lecture to her Taylor peers, Janelle argues the solution to desiring more is working with what you have. "Some of the kids at Taylor, they complain so much: like, 'Oh, Taylor don't do this. Taylor doesn't have this.'" To this way of thinking, she replies, "Act like you go to Wyndham. Act like you go to a well-funded school. When life gives you lemons, make lemonade basically."

There are small ways in which this might be possible: students from anywhere can study and try hard at school. But acting like you have a marine biology class, an assigned college counselor, a social worker, or enough computers and supplies is impossible when these things are simply missing. The Taylor students know this, somewhat; they do recognize the importance of school resources. But the societal expectation of merit against all odds, the desire to assert self-sufficiency and pride, and the impulse to avoid being seen as bitter or selfish are mixed in, too. With that, the Taylor students can talk themselves out of articulating their legitimate school needs.

Already sensitive about Taylor's reputation, being in Wyndham confirmed some students' fears. "I felt like we didn't have nothing to offer because their school is probably better than ours," Jaime said, describing his feelings about the school tours. Earlier, Slim shared a similar emotion, when she said comparing schools feels "kind of embarrassing" because Taylor students "don't want to be the worst." You can see a process here of internalizing a judgment about worth based on their school's reduced resources.

Shame, a worry that "we aren't good enough," can explain a lot of this actually, why Taylor students are reluctant to share their reactions to the suburban school. After translating their wish for greater resources into dark emotions—envy, ungratefulness, selfishness—they feel ashamed at having them, believing that is not who they are supposed to be. After seeing Wyndham, they rate the two schools as "better" and "worse," and feel embarrassed by their ranking. These interpretations lead inward, towards self-criticism and doubt, helping to explain why their outward reactions to Wyndham are so muted. That and just downright shock.

This is ultimately Metro's job to fix because the blame is going to the wrong place. Their character is not impugned when they want what Wyndham has; that is not envy. Their school is not "bad" or "worse" in comparison to Wyndham—it has fewer resources, yes, it is unable to offer the same opportunities—but denigrating self-judgment does not accurately describe the problem. And most of all: the Taylor students are not to blame for the societal flaws that make their school the way it is.

❖

PART II CODA

The Trickiness of Communicating the Educational Divide

I WANT TO BACK UP for a second and recognize how hard this is. Most adults do not have the experience of talking about hard social issues with people who are more and less advantaged than they are. In the Metropolitan Community Project, we are asking kids to do this. Not only that, we're bringing students from opposite sides of the educational divide into the very spaces where they are divided: their unequal schools. The students stand next to each other, looking at the gap in educational opportunity. The contrast is high and very, very real. And then we ask them to talk about it, while they're still there. This is a scary conversation; no wonder they get stuck.

What's interesting is that they're coming from very different social positions but they get stuck in the same places. Both privately worry that their school's status will be confused with their character. Wyndham students are anxious their sizable advantages will make them seem arrogant and clueless about how everyone else lives. Taylor students are afraid their under-resourced city school signifies to outsiders that they are, in their words, "bad" kids who "don't try." Speaking clearly about the other school's circumstances feels to both groups like an insult. To the Wyndham students, it seems like criticizing the city school, and to the Taylor students, it sounds blaming to point out what Wyndham has. Everyone's "embarrassed:" Wyndham students by their school's abundance, Taylor students by having fewer things to show or "offer."

What would you do if you were in this situation? I'm getting a little panicky as I describe all this to you. I kind of want to go hide. With all of this discomfort, embarrassment, and self-doubt, and the worry of insulting other kids, I think they feel a little bit like hiding too. And so, they start saying stuff to shrink the gap. The Wyndham students diminish their school's advantages—"it's not that great"—and emphasize their problems: the stress, the lack of camaraderie, the leaking roof. The Taylor students understate the obstacles—"it isn't that bad"—and highlight their strengths: the community feel, the cultural expression, their success against the odds.

If you squint while they're talking, it's almost as if the schools are the same. Some of the students even say that—"a school is still a school," "it's like every other school."

But then, and this is the concern, we lose track of what we're talking about. Things go all fuzzy. Strengths are washed out by challenges, and challenges are compensated by strengths until it appears everyone's even. But that is not correct. Even with its difficulties, Wyndham, the suburban school, has everything it needs, more than enough, every advantage. And over in the city, with recognition of all of Taylor's assets, the school still has unfilled needs and students facing steep barriers. What gets lost in the midst of all this cautious conversation is educational inequality.

There is some credit due, however, for what's behind the Metro students' elisions. The Wyndham students are not asserting what we hear quite often, that they worked hard for what they have, and hence, they've earned their school resources. When they're self-conscious about excess, when they feel like it isn't merited, that is further along than the general public.

The Taylor students don't completely buy the public's rhetoric about them, either. They rightfully insist on respect—for themselves and for their school—even as they worry about the judgments that may come down on them anyway. And we have to recognize here that for the Taylor students the threat of outsiders' judgments poses a deeper harm. It hurts to be thought of as arrogant or snotty. But being stereotyped as lacking in work ethic or character is an attack on kids of color's humanity. In this context, the Taylor students' pushback is brave and corrective, even as its expression might obscure the barriers they are contending with.

There is also something sweet relationally that is happening when the Wyndham and Taylor students do not wish to offend. They are being sensitive towards each other, approaching their conversations gingerly. They don't want to make anyone feel "less than" or criticized. Some of the insistence that their schools are the same comes from a desire to recognize common humanity. They want to affirm the goodness in each other, and in each other's schools. These are nice intentions, and then they overshoot, by stopping themselves from saying things they mean.

So this is where I want to come back to the students' measure of an open conversation, their use of terms like "honesty" and "truthfulness." These words carry judgment: live up to them and you're a person of sterling character; fall short and you may be lacking in morality. Just looking at the antonyms shows how hard these words can be on people: dishonest, lying, deceitful, false. I think you can agree that when the Taylor and Wyndham students feel unable to fully express their views on each other's schools, or "dim down" the presentation of their own, these words do not apply. I would like to propose, then, that the positive appeals to be honest and truthful do not apply, either. These guidelines miss the emotional work of talking about disparity and the students' intentions to treat each other kindly.

We do want students to communicate what it means to them to travel back and forth between these schools, however. Doing so will bring them closer to understanding the severity and impact of educational disparity, "to know what's the problem," as Slim has said. I've been sprinkling the words "open" and "direct" throughout this section, my attempt to create a more neutral ideal for students' conversations. Setting an intention for direct communication recognizes the trickiness of this kind of talk—the niceties, discomforts, and fears that can impede it—and removes some of the sting of judgment when students get stuck. The opposite of direct is indirect, as in, not saying all that we think or experience. That seems to be about right, from the students' testimony, but it is not a criticism. It's just an opening to find the sticking points, and to learn how to speak more freely with students from the other side of the divide.

❖

Open Communication: The Taylor & Wyndham Students' Public Talk

Let's hear what openness sounds like. These are the rarer conversations, but they're important. They show us the kind of exchange we're hoping for, when the city and suburban students can share opposite experiences and unscripted reactions—when they start to see what's underneath.

This is at lunch, during the Taylor tour day (a Thursday). Lucy, who goes to Taylor, is chatting with Caroline and Elizabeth, visitors from Wyndham.

> Lucy tells Caroline and Elizabeth she has a job at McDonald's. "What do you do there?" asks Caroline. "I'm a cashier and a server," Lucy says, "and my shift ends at midnight." "Oh my gosh!," Caroline reacts. "Is that like

> on a Saturday?" "No, this was last night!," Lucy says. She stayed after to socialize for a bit, and then took the train and a bus home, getting back at 2 in the morning. Caroline asks if Lucy buys her own clothes with the money she makes from her job, and Lucy nods yes.

This is another lunch, this time on the Wyndham tour. Elizabeth and Lucy meet again, along with Taylor students Jaime and Jerry.

> Elizabeth lists the course line-up at Wyndham, typically Math, English, Art, Business, Science, Foreign Language, and Gym. Taylor doesn't require Foreign Language to graduate, Lucy remarks. It's still important, Elizabeth says, because colleges often do.
>
> Jaime asks Elizabeth how she gets to school. Elizabeth replies she would drive but Wyndham's parking spaces cost $500 and are assigned by lottery, making them difficult to get. "If you can't park, do you walk?," Jerry asks. "I have to be here so early that my mom drives me," Elizabeth answers. "I have class at 7:15." "Who goes to class at 7:15?!," Lucy asks incredulously. "About 30% of the school!," Elizabeth replies. "There are so many classes you can take that a lot of students choose to take Gym or Science for zero period." "Hell!," responds Lucy, at the thought of voluntarily going to school before dawn. She thinks for a second, and adds, "I would choose Gym if I had to go early." Elizabeth agrees this is a good choice, because then you can start the day with yoga. Lucy says, "You guys have so many electives. If we had that, I'd look forward to going to school."

These conversations look open to me because they show little windows into life outside of school, capture distinct difference, and contain genuine shock.

In the first scene, Lucy describes how she works many hours, takes public transportation, and gets home late on school nights. Caroline is surprised, and in that surprise, you see a difference: for her, weeknights are for schoolwork, and supplementary income is not required.

In the second scene, we see that Elizabeth's mother takes her to school in the family car, but many Wyndham students drive their own, and that's costly. Elizabeth knows which classes are esteemed by colleges, and she reports that many students are taking a "zero period" to pad their résumés. Plus, you can have a relaxing, healthful start to the school day through yoga. Lucy thinks this is all crazy, and in that reaction, you can also discern a difference: there are fewer curricular options available to her and fewer sources of college knowledge. At the scene's end, Lucy reflects on what opportunities like Elizabeth's would mean for her own education.

I want to think with you about what promotes moments like this, conversations that communicate lived-in experience, and through these different realities, a deeper truth about social and educational inequality. To me, what Metro brings at its best is an infrastructure for building relationships and taking action. And when students feel rooted in that infrastructure, they are freer to engage in more direct talk.

We've already covered how vulnerable the students feel showing their school lives to outsiders. They don't want to get hurt. Before they even meet, they're projecting out what it will look like if things go badly. The worst-case scenario for the students at Wyndham is that the Taylor students will come into their school, see all of their stuff, and get mad—at them. The Taylor students imagine that the Wyndham visitors will bring their haughty attitudes and deem them unworthy.

Then they meet, and continue to talk, over a school year and sometimes more. And gradually, their fears diminish. When Abbey initially pictured Metro in her mind, she worried the Taylor students would react to her suburban school with an accusatory, "'Why do you have that and not us?!'" But instead, they responded calmly with, "'That'd be really cool if we had that.'" The equanimous reaction helped Abbey "feel comfortable" enough to "talk about our differences between our schools."

It's worth saying that the Taylor students have every right to be pissed, and they should be able to express their anger. The educational system discriminates against them, and they are receiving only a fraction of what they should be. The Metropolitan Community Project has more work to do in preparing the suburban students for this justified response, and in increasing their analytical capacity to see that it's directed at the larger system.

Glimmers of that capacity-building appear in the Wyndham students' discovery, upon meeting the Taylor students, that they are not a personal target. Feeling like the Taylor students trust them enough frees up space, for being open about educational disparity, and for admitting their place on the advantaged side of the spectrum. "They were really welcoming to how sensitive this whole topic is for them," Adrianna said, of the students from Chicago. "I don't think it's nearly as sensitive to me, because I guess I have a little bit of the upper hand in this" school system, societally speaking.

The Taylor students were sensitive about this topic, as we know. They worried the suburban kids might act superior, "like stuck up people," as Lucy put it, and assume the worst about the city school and the students who went there. They paid attention, warily, to how the Wyndham students treated them when they visited. When things went better than they'd imagined, their apprehensions started to subside. In real life, the suburban kids acted like "normal students that just have a little more than we do," Lucy said, belying her fears. Seeing that the Wyndham students didn't hold themselves apart allowed more vulnerability to emerge. Slim was at first "uncomfortable talking about how different it is" at Taylor. "But they seemed really open and friendly," she said, after meeting the Wyndham kids. "And it's like you could tell them the truth about it." The open-mindedness she encountered created more openness on her part.

Going on a scavenger hunt. Photo courtesy of author.

The ease and comfort the students began to feel with each other had a lot to do with the amount of time they spent together. The Metropolitan Community Project goes for a whole year, with an initial meeting, tours at each school, and planning for an educational action. By the time we get to the end, the communication gets a little bolder. Janelle from Taylor narrates this arc:

> In the beginning of the year, of course, we were more isolated, because we were coming from different backgrounds: different school backgrounds and different community backgrounds. So we kind of had our guards up. But working together, we had a chance to open up. We got a little peace of mind and personality out of everyone. And that way our bond between Wyndham and Taylor became stronger.

For Janelle, the instinctive reaction to encountering so much difference was to have your guard up, to hold back. Time and collaboration changed that, helping students share their thoughts and perspectives more fully.

Maya was in Janelle's group and traveled exactly this route. She was one of the Wyndham students who told me of her impulse to shorten her school tour because she was afraid of making the Taylor students feel bad. And she intentionally didn't say what she felt Taylor was "lacking" in front of them. During the tours, though, "we didn't really know them as well, so I feel we were a little bit more shy and tried not to be so honest." By the end of the year, "I think now I could. I've gotten so much more comfortable with Janelle and Slim that I could say to them, 'You don't have this, and we do.' And they could say, 'You guys have everything' and I'd be like, 'ok.'" Her communication shifted from circumspect, indirect talk to a clear acknowledgement of disparity and a simple admission of her privilege. The way through for Maya, and for many other Metro students, was the time to form personal relationships with kids on the other side of the divide.

The time factor played an even stronger role when Metro students participated in the project for multiple years. This is partly what explains the rapport of Elizabeth and Lucy, the Wyndham and Taylor students who appear at the beginning of this segment. Elizabeth told me, "it took a little bit" to get comfortable "because it's like you're meeting this brand new person," and, as she said earlier, "emphasizing the differences between us" felt hard. But "I was with Lucy most of the year," and eventually, "we could open up. Once you start talking, it was ok." By her second year, the two were planning sleepovers to extend the exchange experience.

All their bonding led to some remarkably open sharing. With Elizabeth, Lucy told me, "We talked about how her mom is a teacher, and her dad is a doctor. How they don't struggle economically-wise and how they have a big house" in the suburbs. Elizabeth got a peek inside Lucy's home life too.

"It's very different. She has 13 people in a three-bedroom apartment" in Chicago, Elizabeth recalled. "She has to go to work, and take a train and a bus to get there and back."

It was easier to converse this way after the time spent getting to know each other. And it didn't always have to be serious. "We talked about what we do for fun," (Lucy), and boyfriends (Elizabeth), so it was "not just a focus on like, '*oh*, school funding.'"

When school funding and its constraints did come up, it helped that they'd talked about the topic before. "I guess it felt a little better because this is my second year," Trina told me, after taking the Wyndham students on a tour through her school. It felt less sensitive to reveal the limit side of disparity once she'd established some comfort with the suburban students. Her goal now, she said, was to show "mainly the huge differences that we could actually see, like the size of our libraries."

Slim, who was adamant that "both sides need to be more honest" about their schools, got some of that courage from doing Metro three years in a row. "Since I was already used to some of them," she said, meaning the Wyndham students, "I felt it was a really good interaction." By the time she gave her third tour of Taylor, "I kind of told them what they're going to be looking at. I was like: 'This is going to be completely different.'" As the kids got "used to" each other, their fears receded, creating space to talk intentionally about difference.

The other space-opening opportunity for real conversations about difference was activism. Having a purpose for experiencing all this upsetting disparity helped the Taylor and Wyndham students keep talking.

For the Taylor students, learning about the suburban school cut deep. Participating in Metro, "made me angry," Ailany said. While the suburban students "had it all in their school," hers consisted of classes with "30 other students and not enough books." Anger can cut people off, can make them recede. But when I asked Ailany, "What do you do with that anger?," she replied, "I do stuff like join this program, and I try to inform other people about it, and make a difference in it." Ailany channeled her emotions into a search for change, engaging directly with inequality in the process.

More worrying, perhaps, than anger, Xavia responded to the disparity she saw with intense sadness, feeling like she was shut out of opportunity.

Seeing Wyndham for the first time "really put me down," she said. "You could see the unfairness." Yet rather than falling into self-doubt, Xavia externalized these feelings into an activist identity. She came back to Metro for another year, and at the end, as she was about to graduate, she reflected on her initial reaction. "It just hit me that I didn't get the best quality of education my whole life, 18 years of life," she said. But instead of feeling "bad, it's got me more, if anything, feisty. I'm just really pumped up. So I'll become a teacher, and I'll speak about this, and like, I'll spit at politicians." (She said this last part in a kidding but "feisty" way.)

The emotions that held the Wyndham students back from direct talk were permutations of defensiveness and guilt. In her community, Caitlin observed, it was common to take "privileged" as "an insult, which it's not." Her way of not rising to that reaction was to say to herself, "You should be happy that you have these advantages, but you should also be aware that other people don't, and try to help bridge the gap." Abbey similarly gave herself a talking-to when self-consciousness built up over all she had in her school. She reminded herself that "if I could have it my way, I would have equality in the school system." She defused the inner tension by committing to this larger purpose.

Knowing the other students stood with them also made it easier to talk about the gap. Allie started out unsure that the suburban students could relate to her experience. "You have the Wyndham kids: they already have everything." But she discovered, "they still think it's unequal for us to not have the same things they do. When we tell them, 'well, we don't have this, but you do,' they say, 'oh, really?'" Their surprise and concern helped her open up about her school's challenges. It made the differences between them seem like less of a divide.

Like many Wyndham students, Noa felt "uncomfortable," knowing her suburban school was "better off" and seeing "how upset" the Taylor students could be. "How did you deal with that discomfort when it happened?," I asked her. "We thought about it," she answered. "They know that we care. We're in the project together, so they know we want the same things they do." The "same" goal was educational equality, and the sense that they were in it together, to try to achieve that end, helped them cross the boundary.

And in the Metropolitan Community Project, the wish for equality doesn't stay abstract. The kids' ideals, and their growing sense of solidarity, have a concrete place to go. A happy byproduct of our organizing was more open conversation about difference.

Picture, for example, one of our action prep days, courtesy of Rusty, a student from Taylor. The Metro students were composing letters to their state legislators, and chatting about what to write as they went:

> The letter-writing that we did, we were in our groups, some Wyndham students, some Taylor students. And we got to see how their public school life was for elementary school. And how, at Taylor, people from around here, we had to supply our school with paper, paper towels, toilet paper, soap. And they didn't have to do anything like that. But we did, and that just made, like, a very eye-opening point.

Here, they exchanged very small details of their school experience, whose simplicity—a difference of toilet paper and soap—provided an "eye-opening" view of educational disparity.

It mattered to both the suburban and city students that they had a venue to do this in, that they weren't comparing just to compare. It helped to tamp down some of the emotions that could otherwise block a more open interchange. Jonas told me, "It was kind of hard at first to talk about the differences. I think it was because of the guilt we felt," as Wyndham students. But then he realized, "the project was really a constructive way to change and make these kinds of opportunities available at Taylor. Once that sank in, I was able to talk about the differences. I knew whatever I said, I can help testify in Springfield, help someone know more about educational inequality." The discomfort of acknowledging privilege did not totally subside, but it had a positive outlet.

The Taylor students weren't dealing with guilt, but they were working through what it meant to see their school anew and wish that they had what the wealthier school provides. The opportunity to take action helped them process these realizations. "I learned a lot, I think my mind has opened out," Mia told me, after participating in Metro. At Wyndham, "they get more money" was the first thing on the list. "I also learned Taylor could be a lot better, but it's not, and it's just something that we could change." There is no shame, embarrassment, or self-blame being expressed here. Instead, Mia levels-up from these personal reactions, thinking about a system that is wrong, and actions that could help make it right. Also, she says improving schools like Taylor is "something we could change," as in, the suburban students and me, we can make that possible.

A collaborative vision like this made hard conversations easier, more purposeful. They were talking for a reason. "It felt very safe and very open to discuss," Maggie from Wyndham ultimately felt, because "it's a problem that we—on both sides—want to come up with a solution for, and we want to move forward." Sharing in the work for a "solution" made the things they didn't have in common feel safer.

So these were the things that helped them move through the hard parts of their conversations: growing relationships, working towards change. The bonds they formed, and the purpose-driven nature of their talk, encouraged more openness. When they knew each other better, when they had a commitment to change in common, *when they did the work*, they could speak more directly about the educational gulf between them. They could talk through their guilt, anger, and sadness, and take these feelings out on the system instead. It wasn't always that the city and suburban students could do this. But it was their connection, and their political engagement, that made the difference when they could.

You'll get to see this in the next chapter, too, how much their wariness falls away when talk of disparity is paired with advocacy. Their observations suddenly turn crisp. The Taylor students say what they would borrow from Wyndham and why. They express unmet needs. The Wyndham students are surprised by what Taylor is missing, and say so, out loud. They admit to what they have and how much it helps. As the city and suburban kids talk, the educational divide comes into view. Together they show how, if their needs and resources were matched, the system could be whole. The chance to persuade decision-makers with real power is like a release to speak plainly, about the inequality they've witnessed, and the need for change.

❖

PART III

Educational Activism

CHAPTER FIVE

The Students & the Legislators

Planning for Action

Explode these patterns of who we hear from.

—Senator Joseph Bauer (IL-D)

SENATOR JOSEPH BAUER SLIPS quietly into the circle and sits down in an empty seat.[1] Upwards of 50 Metro students surround him. Ms. Isabel, the community organizer, designates the assembly a peace circle: an activity designed to "equalize" conversation and encourage careful listening. A talking piece will be passed around clockwise, and only the person holding it can speak. Earlier, she'd mentioned she picked this approach intentionally, so the legislator couldn't dominate the conversation. So he'd actually hear what the students have to say.

Ms. Isabel begins with a question: "During this project, what did you see or hear about the resources available, or not available, at the other school? And how did that make you feel?"

Annaliese from Wyndham gets the talking piece first. "What really struck me was the lack of human resources at Taylor," she says. "When people actually need a nurse, and they can't have it? It was like, culture-shock." She passes the talking piece to her classmate Laila, who says she was startled "to hear that college counseling is one guy in a room full of computers" when at her school there are "five or six college counselors." Someone from Wyndham shouts "eight!" as a correction. This is technically a rule violation since they're not holding the talking piece.

Later in the circle, Allie from Taylor shares, "I think it's nice how many people they have to help students if they need any help. For college, it's not just one person. The nurse's office, not just limited people." Andy, Allie's friend from Taylor, follows with, "I think the advisory" at Wyndham "would be great for our school. We only have one counselor. We need someone who knows us. We can push ourselves too. But if we saw we had help, we could reach our goals easier."

You've heard some of these issues before, but this time they're being talked about in front of a state senator. Once everyone in the circle has spoken, all eyes turn to Senator Bauer. He's a liberal senator from the northern suburbs, and when he begins to speak, he directs his comments to "my Wyndham friends" first. "What we hear most often," he says, "is that being successful is about innate abilities and talent. The resources are left out." This occurs because school supports are so ubiquitous at Wyndham they become invisible, "no different than breathing air" to the students who go there. The testimony of the Metro students, Senator Bauer argues, shows the meritocratic 'up from your bootstraps' line to be untrue. At schools like Wyndham, resources support students' success and catch them when they falter. At schools like Taylor, "in a resource-constrained environment," even highly motivated students can "fall through the cracks." Senator Bauer concedes that the role of "resource inequalities" is known to lawmakers on a conceptual level. But, he argues, "me and my colleagues need to be reminded by the people who live it."

The reason a reminder is needed is because "we legislators are surrounded by people who have resources," and he admits wealthier constituents "shape our worldview." Changing the system begins with trying to "explode these patterns of who we hear from," and expose legislators to the kind of testimony he's just heard.

Senator Bauer offers this advice on "how to make a difference," to turn the heads and hearts of elected officials: Each student in the Metropolitan Community Project should compose a handwritten letter with the same kind of "intimate, human-level" experiences that were shared today. The letters should be assembled into a packet and sent to all 177 state legislators, along with a request for a meeting. He estimates the number of replies will be modest, perhaps just seven appointments will result. But if the supportive lawmakers "know who each other are," then "it's a start of a movement within the legislature" to begin "progressing in a sane direction."

Once Senator Bauer leaves, it's the students' turn to decide on next steps. Ms. Isabel uses the peace circle process to help them come to consensus on an issue-focus and an action strategy. They're asked which issue is the "biggest injustice" for them, and which one makes most sense for "Wyndham and Taylor to partner and work together on." The kids consider school funding and standardized testing, the latter because the Taylor students feel their school is being penalized unfairly for its scores. In this and subsequent in-school meetings, the Metro students ultimately decide to organize a campaign on school funding, and to adopt the letter-writing strategy.

To help the Metro students prepare, we hold another field trip at an old church in Chicago, in a meeting space empty on weekdays.

A Wyndham teacher, Mr. Bartel, gives a primer on school funding, covering property taxes, the very limited contributions of the state, and how resources become so unequal. He discusses possible reforms, like increasing the state's education budget and requiring wealthier communities to pay a larger share. Another teacher from Wyndham provides tips on how to write an effective letter.

Next, Mr. Rafael, a youth organizer in Taylor's neighborhood, models the tactic of sharing a "story of self" with elected officials. The centerpiece, he says, is a specific, personal experience the audience can relate to that can generate empathy for a larger social issue. The end of the story always includes an "ask"—a concrete action the storyteller wants the decision-maker to take.

As a project, the Metro students have already chosen to take action on school funding, and to contact their state legislators. The intention for today, Mr. Rafael says, is to write a personal story about school and the Metropolitan Community Project that illustrates the problem of educational inequality. "Your reactions to what you've experienced in the project, and your clarity on what's right, is a tactic," Ms. Isabel adds.

Jashaundra wonders what the "ask" at the end of the letter will be. The Metro students and their teachers craft it together: "Will you please meet with us to discuss ways Illinois could strive for more equitable funding in education?"

The kids sit down at big round tables, mixed together, Wyndham and Taylor, and start writing (and talking). We take a pizza break, and they write some more. Ms. Isabel calls everyone together, and we move chairs into a semi-circle. She asks for volunteers from both schools to read. There are a lot of poignant, personal details about school; about advantage and need; about the shock of witnessing schools on the other side of the divide. At the end of every letter comes the same ask, and when it's read aloud, the Metro kids nod and smile in recognition, the pile-up of similar requests creating a kind of momentum.

❖

Dear Legislator,

My name is Mia, and I go to Taylor High School. THS, as it is known by most, is on the Northside of Chicago where many homes have been taken away and where police cars cruise by "just to check on us". I have been working on the Metro Community Project for the past school year. Joining two completely different schools like THS and Wyndham has brought a different point of view to all of us. Although our mission is to fix the differences between the inequalities, we can't get much done without your help.

As a student of the Chicago Public Schools, I've always thought I was getting the best education or at least the same education as others. At THS, needless to say, we are underresourced, but that never bothered me because I though maybe it was normal that the library was never available to us, or that we didn't have any cooking classes, or dance classes, or that our councilers were always too busy to see us. For a second, I even thought that kids getting arested in school was O.k. Yet its not O.k, none of it. I understand that if you go to a paid private school & you'll probably get a fancy education, but I don't understand how having money has anything to do with Public education. Meeting with Wyndham has helped me realize that school funding is a big deal and that we must fight for equality, so that maybe everyone could have an equal opportunity.

I hope you understand the seriousness of this problem, and will concider meeting with us. So, Will you meet with us to begin discussing ways Illinois can strive for more equitable funding in public education?

Sincerely,

Mia

Action Supplies

Here's another advantage to suburban schooling: there's a copy room. It has three huge, industrial-sized machines with sorting and stapling functions. Stashes of envelopes, postage, and printer paper are free for the taking. You'd think these would be small details to mention but they're not. The single machine at Taylor is often out-of-order, and teachers get memos about paper allotments, buying extra with their own money when they max out. So it's not surprising we're at Wyndham to create 177 packets of student letters. Mr. Bartel promises the school "won't even notice" the 'missing' office supplies.

We organize the letters in the packet to go Taylor-Wyndham-Taylor-Wyndham, so if the legislators read them straight through, they'll get the direct contrasts. We co-write a cover letter that includes the Metro facilitators' contact information. We put huge stacks of envelopes in Wyndham campus mail. And we wait.

Not that long, actually. Aides start calling us back pretty quickly. We get about 15 responses from legislators this way. We're relaying the tally to the Metro students as they come in. Most represent districts in the Chicago metro area but a few come from rural regions, in southern and western Illinois, as well as from towns in the far northern part of the state. A few will be too far to get to.

We start arranging meetings. Because it's the end of the session, the legislators are racing to finish work on various bills, and they're in Springfield during the week. The meetings will need to be in the summer, when their time is freer and we can meet in their district offices, closer to Chicago.

❖

Taking Action for Equitable School Funding

Legislators are skilled talkers, and they know how to fill up space to avoid a challenge. Ms. Isabel, with all her experience in youth organizing, had seen this a thousand times: students being rhetorically patted on the head and run over with words by officials intent on grandstanding. Without advanced planning, she knew the Metro students could go into a meeting and realize only afterwards that they'd barely spoken with their representatives. And so, Ms. Isabel created a meeting format to center students' voices: Opening the meeting with each student, in round-robin style, sharing something about their own school's resources and the resources of their Metro partners. Moving to their "asks:" what they want to know from the legislator, and what they want her to do. Closing the meeting with another round-robin on what educational equality means to them. Throughout, returning to what they know: their schools and their firsthand observations of disparity.

We have a process in place but with the first meeting approaching, the Taylor teacher, Mr. Ryan, has to cajole kids to come. When he asks why they're hesitant, Janelle admits, "I don't feel like I know enough about the issue," and Rusty replies, "I don't know what to say." Mr. Ryan tries to assure them: "Yes you do. You've seen the differences. If you just talk about your experiences and speak from the heart, it will go great." But they're fretful they don't have the expertise to speak with someone so important. Katie agrees to come, and Rusty finally does too, literally as we're pulling out of the school parking lot. We're headed to the north suburbs to meet with state representative Claire Orlov.

❖

Chicago already spends significantly more.
—Representative Claire Orlov (IL-D)

In the car, I tell Katie and Rusty a little bit about Representative Orlov: the bills she's sponsored, the committees she serves on. Then, the students practice on me, sharing personal examples from Taylor and thoughts about Wyndham. For asks, they consider various options, from fact-finding questions to more forceful questions about what she's willing to commit to.

Mr. Bartel and the Wyndham students meet us in the parking lot, and we all head inside. The district office has faux wood paneling and old campaign posters taped to the walls. Representative Orlov enters the office while talking through headphones. We stand awkwardly, waiting. After a few minutes, she hangs up and motions us to sit.

At the conference table, the Metro students each take a turn describing the differences they've seen between their schools. They touch on college counseling, libraries, leadership, and access to technology. The representative takes up just one difference out of the many she's heard—principal turnover—and wonders aloud if this is a "commitment issue or a resource issue." Veiled in her question is a claim that flawed individuals rather than unequal systems are to blame for the conditions of city schools.

Mr. Bartel redirects, arguing that consistent staffing is a resource issue. Rusty from Taylor quickly agrees, telling Representative Orlov that she had three different substitute teachers for English her freshman year, each with little subject-area knowledge or experience. When she got to sophomore English, "I didn't know as much as the other students who had the same teacher all year. I was behind and I had to catch up."

Representative Orlov listens and nods, but she also says, "My understanding is that Chicago already spends significantly more than other districts. It may be about allocating limited resources better in that district." Representative Orlov is disputing the assertion of inequality, this time blaming the city school system. And the statement she makes is inaccurate: Chicago Public Schools' funding is near the state average while Wyndham, and districts like it, have $10,000 more to devote to every student, every year. On top of this, Chicago serves the highest-need students in the state, making the missing dollars even more critical. When a conversation starts this way, there's probably a tough meeting ahead.

The students move to the "ask" portion of the meeting. Laila from Wyndham wants to know, "Where are there conversations about this issue in the state legislature?" Representative Orlov replies, "Nowhere. They aren't happening." She tells us the state is in the middle of budget cutbacks and trying to fund public employee pensions. "So funding equity isn't even on the radar." A task force was recently formed to study the issue, but the members have not been chosen. She suggests the students apply more pressure to state government, to encourage them to act. Asked how, she recommends social media strategies.

Shana asks, "We're talking to other legislators about this. Would you be willing to join a coalition of other legislators on school funding equity?" Representative Orlov answers she'll think about it, which seems like a no. She explains that education is "not one of the main issues I work on." She's been very polite this whole time, if a little cold.

The energy in the room starts to flag, so the students begin their closing remarks, on why educational equality matters to them. The Taylor students go first. "It matters," Rusty says, "because it's my education. We need the same opportunities." Katie considers the nationwide implications: "I think this is about the country. If we create an equal education system, the whole country will be stronger." Shana from Wyndham says the quality of a student's education should not be based on where that student is born. "It's not right," Annaliese tells Representative Orlov, that young people should "be so worried" about "having a high-quality education." We thank the representative and say our goodbyes.

The students debrief.

On the car ride home, I ask Rusty and Katie about their experience. Katie calls Representative Orlov, "truthful," adding, "you need people like that. It's better than people saying everything will be perfect and we'll fix the problem." Rusty agrees. "You don't want people to lie to you," she says.

It's funny; I took the conversation way harder than they did. I was closer to Mr. Bartel, who found it "disheartening" because the legislator left so little hope, almost to the point of resistance, when "there are futures at stake." But the Taylor kids found the bleak delivery refreshing, appreciating that someone in her position could be so direct.

Yet, when I ask, "How did you guys feel when she said you needed to wait until the state had enough money?" Rusty answers, "How did I feel? I felt bad. It was horrible. We come last even though it's an important issue." So maybe it's one thing to tell it like it is, but it's another thing to show city youth how low a priority their state government makes them.

I remind Rusty she was nervous going into the meeting. Once she was there though, she spoke out strongly. Rusty says, "I had to. They were so . . ." Her voice trails off. I don't know what she means, but Katie does. "I know, they seemed to know so much more about the senate."

They're referring to the Wyndham students: their confidence debating a legislator on educational policy. Rusty thinks the difference in their interaction styles helps to illustrate why they were in the representative's office in the first place. "I think it's good that she heard us like that. Not to knock us down, but I think they get a higher education than us, and you can see the impact it has on us and our learning." The hurt in Rusty's reflection shows just how vulnerable the Taylor students feel during these actions for change—and how brave they are to show up and give their testimony anyway.

To challenge their views a little though, I think Rusty and Katie are being too hard on themselves. There may be some differences in background knowledge that help to explain the differing comfort levels. But the suburban students' assurance is also about a society that values wealth and privilege, and the sense of power that flows from that. When I ask Jashaundra from Wyndham afterwards, she tells me she was nervous at the meeting, too. But tellingly she refers to the representative as "Claire," as if they are on a first-name basis, as if their statuses are similar.

The next meeting with a legislator is also a tale of pushback, of inequality minimized.

❖

It's not that different.
—Representative Patrick Knight (IL-D)

Representative Patrick Knight's district is a set of neighborhoods on the north side of Chicago, some wealthy and some mixed- to lower-income but rapidly gentrifying. He is best known for being the first out gay legislator in Illinois, and for courageously sponsoring and pushing through a bill legalizing gay marriage in the state before it was legalized nationally by the Supreme Court. Indeed, when we arrive at his office, his staff is assembling huge piles of supplies for the Pride March to occur that weekend. He is an outspoken advocate for gay rights but from our meeting appears to have some blind spots on other kinds of equity.

We can see this from the opening moments of the meeting with Representative Knight, when the Metro students try to illustrate their disparate educations. Jashaundra compares the schools' libraries, saying Wyndham's contains "multiple rooms and it's always available" while the Taylor library "is only one room" and is frequently "not available."

Representative Knight asks how many students attend each school, and when he hears Taylor has a smaller student body, he suggests that the library's size is merely a function of numbers. The Metro students rush to

Dear State Legislator:

My name is **Jade**, and I am a junior at **Wyndham** High School. I moved to the North Shore Chicago almost three years ago, an area that I knew very little about. This school year, I have had the opportunity to participate in the Metropolitan Community Project, getting to know other high school students from a neighborhood school in Chicago and learning about how drastic inequities in Illinois public school funding affect us all in our daily lives.

Although I have attended a variety of schools in my life, I have always been lucky enough to have excellent academic experiences. Whenever we moved to a new place, my parents chose their new zip code based on the quality of the school district. I never thought too much about how my education would be different if my parents didn't have the economic freedom necessary to send me to the public schools of their choice. At **Wyndham**, I was both overwhelmed and impressed by the array of curricular and extracurricular choices. I was always aware that schools in Chicago were radically different as a result of inadequate school funding, but I never knew what those concrete differences looked like until I began the Metropolitan Community Project.

When working on the project, I was most struck by how much we at **Wyndham** take our abundance of human resources fir granted. I knew that funding impacted the number of teachers and counselors a school could hire, but I honestly never considered how a strong system of advisers, social workers, and college counselors make a school environment more stable and safe. My peers from **Taylor** opened my eyes to this, commenting on how they wished their school had,

I now agree with them that we want to help such a safety net is essential if students reach their full potential. a tighter safety net that would not allow individuals to fall through the cracks. In high school, it is easy for anyone, including me, to feel anonymous, unnoticed, and invisible. I can only imagine that it would only be easier in a school that gives fewer second chances to struggling students and offers fewer avenues for support.

This is only one example of the complex relationship between school funding and school environment. I now realize, and I hope you do as well, that we need to reevaluate how we as a state can best support schools that meet the needs of our communities and all their young members. ~~To begin this discussion~~, I just have one question: will you meet with us to begin discussing ways Illinois can strive for more equitable funding in education?

Thank you for your time,

Jade

counteract this idea: "It's still not sufficient, even for the size of Taylor," argues Annaliese from Wyndham. Katie, who's from Taylor adds, "Our library is also our computer lab. Even if we can use the library, it's loud because the teacher is giving directions. So there's never a quiet space and we have difficulty getting our work done."

But Representative Knight lets the library and studying concerns drop. Even though the students are telling him the Chicago library does not offer enough books, space, or study time.

This happens again. Jerry from Taylor notes, "Our classes are packed with large numbers of students," often more than 30. He tells the representative how "difficult" it is for his teachers to "focus on all of them" and "to push each one of them."

Representative Knight responds with a question: "How many students are there per class at Wyndham?" Annaliese answers, "About 20." Representative Knight remarks the class sizes are "not too far apart," minimizing the difference and the Taylor students' experiences, not to mention all of the research showing how class size matters for achievement (e.g., Mosteller, 1995).

A little later, Annaliese tells Representative Knight, "One thing you should know about Wyndham is our advisory system." The advisor is an advocate, counselor, and college guide who stays with the same small cohort of students all four years, meeting with them every day. "There's no one at Taylor" in a role quite like this, Annaliese adds. Mr. Bartel explains the system is "expensive," because teachers receive a course release to become an advisor.

Representative Knight asks how many classes teachers teach at each school. When he hears a similar number, he says, "So it's not that different." But advisors teach one fewer class. More importantly, there are personal advisors available to the suburban students while the Chicago school gets one college counselor for the entire student body. Representative Knight, though, does not return to the advising resource, or the extra funding that makes this possible, after his declaration.

> He's obviously very knowledgeable, and policy-wise, he supports increasing the state's contribution to school funding, and even changing the tax structure to do that. So he believes there's a problem and is supportive of a

relatively progressive solution, but he doesn't call it equity. It's about more money for education, but not so much about closing a gap, a gap that doesn't feel as big or as gut-level unfair to him as the students express it to be.

The students debrief.

Or that was my reading. Katie afterwards reacts, "He's such a nice guy!" Jerry agrees, observing, "he was nice and open, and it wasn't that hard to talk to him." Both students feel he listened to them, and both believe he will do something about school funding.

So maybe I'm just sensitive, but I'm surprised again—by the legislators' technical-bureaucratic-debating approach, by their seeming deflection of very personal experience with unequal opportunity.

The meeting with Senator Sonya Cowan stands apart, mostly because of this: empathy.

❖

You're here for school funding equality! Yeah!
—Senator Sonya Cowan (IL-D)

Senator Cowan represents the south and west sides of Chicago, the city's predominantly Black and lower-income neighborhoods, as well as a few south-suburban areas that are diverse and working class. It takes about 40 minutes to get to her office from Taylor and over an hour from Wyndham. To fit into Senator Cowan's schedule, the Taylor group has to leave before last period, and the Wyndham students can't get there in time. So it's just Allie, Andy, and me going to the meeting. On the way, I tell them that Senator Cowan is vice-chair of the education committee and an assistant majority leader in the Senate. We park at a small office building and head inside.

We know we're in the right place when we see a glass door engraved with the Illinois state seal. When I open the door, Allie blurts out, "I'm so nervous! I'm so nervous!" I do some reassuring, reminding Allie the senator asked to meet with us.

Senator Cowan enters the waiting room a few minutes later, and by chance, greets Allie first. "Hello! Who are you?," she asks. Allie shrinks down and whispers, "Allie?" Senator Cowan exclaims, "It's nice to meet you!" and envelops her in a hug. She hugs Andy, too. Even I get one. She shows the three of us into her office and tells us where to sit: the students on the couch, Senator Cowan and myself in leather chairs facing them.

Between us is a coffee table with photography books on Michelle and Barack Obama; an enormous painting of an African American woman in prayer hangs on one wall. An aide enters and hands Senator Cowan a file folder, which she opens. Inside is a notepad, a summary of the project, and the Metro students' letters. Senator Cowan glances over the packet and shouts happily, "You're here for school funding equality!" She waves her hands in the air. "Yeah! This is right up my alley. That's what I've been fighting for, for years!"

Senator Cowan pauses to give the students a chance to speak. Allie starts in, with a description of the school differences that matter to her. She talks about the "huge library" at Wyndham, and the "really small" one at Taylor. Once, when her school library didn't have a book for an assignment, she had to go to two different public libraries to find it. "It was frustrating because I was trying to finish my work, and I didn't have what I needed."

Senator Cowan is taking notes.

There are "really new computers" at Wyndham, Allie continues, unlike the "really old" ones at her school that "take a half-hour to turn on." Also, "my classes kept getting switched around" at the beginning of this year, but when she tried to "go see my counselor to get it fixed, she's not there."

When Allie is finished, Senator Cowan agrees that good libraries are important, and acknowledges her frustration at having to go to so many places to find what she needs. Allie smiles and nods.

"What really gets me," Andy says, going next, "is all year, almost all we've done is get ready for the ACT. At Wyndham, the students told us, they don't have to do that unless they want to, and they do it outside of school."

Taking more notes, Senator Cowan recaps, "So there's an over-emphasis on standardized testing?" Andy answers, "Yes." Senator Cowan says she agrees testing has become too much a part of the curriculum in struggling schools.

Andy switches to a new topic. "Another thing is, we only have two gyms. At Wyndham they have . . ." She pauses and looks at me. "Five?" I hold up my fingers to count 10, and Senator Cowan and Andy both laugh. Andy says, "I'm on the soccer team and we don't have a place to train, because both gyms are taken with other sports. We run in the hallway and outside. At Wyndham, they have an indoor track. Another thing: we have to share uniforms with the guys' soccer team." Senator Cowan reacts, "Ugh! Who would want to share a uniform with a guy?!" Andy adds, "And you can't get the smell out of the uniforms."

Senator Cowan responds to Andy's testimony with, "I can see why you need more space. How nice it would be to have a soccer gym, and your own uniforms." She pauses and says to both students, "Thank you for sharing your stories."

This is so different from the meetings that have come before. She sounds genuinely appalled at the sweaty uniforms, concerned about testing, and understanding of the library restrictions. She acknowledges the emotional side of educational constraint: the frustrations and disappointments students experience in a system that offers too little.

Perhaps this gives Andy courage, because she takes charge. "With all that being said, are you willing to join in a group with other senators to do something about making funding more equal?"

Senator Cowan tells Andy she already is. She and a downstate rural legislator recently started a task force to look at reforming school funding in the state. Before, she felt like she was out there fighting "all by myself," but "now I'm more hopeful" because other parts of the state are realizing "we have a lot of the same problems."

There are numerous challenges to solving them: "finding the money" for education in a time of cutbacks, the pension crisis, and political resistance. "It will take a while," Senator Cowan says, to meet these challenges and gather support, "but we really need to make sure that education is funded." "And equal," Andy adds forcefully. "And equal," Senator Cowan repeats, nodding in agreement.

I know the students want to talk about how to get to equality, so I remind them gently: "What did you guys learn about how schools are funded?" Allie and Andy say in unison: "property taxes." Andy adds, looking at Senator Cowan, "their houses are really big," a remark on the size of suburban homes and the amount of money raised. Senator Cowan laughs and promises the task force will look into moving away from this method of funding schools.

In addition to local funds, Andy tells Senator Cowan that she learned that the state provides about $600 to each Wyndham student even though they live in a wealthy area. On one of our field trips, Andy says, "The students at Wyndham were saying, 'We don't even need it. Why don't we give it back?'"

Senator Cowan observes this offer means the Metro students have found "a common ground," and she compliments Andy and Allie for "creating relationships." The state legislature, by contrast, is "too divided," she says. Legislators "need their own coalitions," their own Metropolitan Community Project.

Senator Cowan excuses herself briefly to make a phone call. In the meantime, Allie works up the courage to ask one last question. When Senator Cowan returns, Allie asks her, "Do you think things will ever change, even if it takes a long time?"

Senator Cowan replies, "I hope so. I gave myself 20 years in the Senate, and I have four more to go. So at least now I know we're on a 30-year plan. And you guys will be, what, graduating from college? And it has to be an issue you're willing to lose over. I'm willing, but not many people are. When people are running for election, they say they care about education in those mailers. But then they get to the legislature, and it's clear that they don't."

Senator Cowan pledges to Andy and Allie, "I'm going to keep fighting." She tells them she's taken notes during the conversation, and she will include their testimony in her next speech from the Senate floor.

Before we go, Senator Cowan gives Andy and Allie a little pep talk on their own education, telling them to study hard and do well in school. "You will go to college," she states emphatically. "I'm talking to you like I talk to my nieces. You are going to go."

We stand up to leave, and the students move to shake Senator Cowan's hand. She hugs them instead. Leaving the office, Allie and Andy take about half the candy from the jar in the waiting room, for the road.

Dear State Legislator:

My name is Allie. I'm 17 years old and I'm a junior at Taylor Highschool. I have proudly been part of the Metro community project for 2 years. What has led me to write this letter is the inequalities between schools and how we all have diffrent ways of learning because of resources we have or dont have. Being in the Metro community project really made me see alot of huge diffrences between schools. Ive realized we are all funded diffrently and we have diffrent resources. Being able to expirience this through the Metro Community Project has led me to write this letter.

When I first went to Taylor Highschool I thought the school was huge and we had good things to work with that was until one of my teachers said he couldnt bealieve how he cant get get computers for us to work on because they were reserved. Thats when I started noticing these diffrences. I thought It was normal for that to happen because the school had only so many children. Ive had also come to a point Where I would try to talk to my Councelor but she was either busy or she wasnt in her office.

Ive stopped thinking it was normal when I was a Sophmore and Joined the Metro Community Project.

where I leared all the diffrences.
This year I joined this project again
and we have seen huge diffrences with
Wyndham and **Taylor** highschool.
Wyndham doesnt have to worry
about reserving computer rooms or if
the person they need is there or not to
help them because they are always
there for them.

Being exposed to all these diffrences
is really sad. Not being able to use
resources because your teacher has to
reserve them is really dissapointing or
not being able to seek help from staff
when you need them in the building
is not good at all. This is why Mr. Senator
I am writing to you. I also would like
to ask you if you would please
meet with us to begin dissussing
ways Illinois can strive for more
equitable funding for education.
I really hope you meet with us because
I bealieve we all deserve an equal
education it doesnt have to matter
who we are or where we live,
all we want is to learn in
a good learning environment.

Sincerely,

Allie

The students debrief.

"I thought it was going to be hard," Allie said later, to talk to Senator Cowan, "since she's up there" in terms of position and status. But "it was pretty easy. I guess because she was very nice." Plus, it helped that "she was talking about things that were the same as we said" and agreed "that had to be changed." These weren't just words, Allie thought. "She really meant that she wanted a change." Andy believed so too. "She seemed sincere." They'd found an ally.

But was this enough? From what it sounded like during the meeting, "she's the only one fighting," Allie worried. Even though, "you'd think, if it's the senate, everyone would be working on this."

You would think that, if you trusted the political process and the priorities of those in power. But Andy didn't. The political system is racially unequal, Andy observed. "She's still considered a minority," as an African American woman, "even if she is a senator." The power structure in the state, predominated by white men, meant "people will still not take her serious," Andy stated. So while Andy trusted Senator Cowan was with them, she didn't think the senator by "herself" had "enough power" in the legislature to effect change.

A meeting with only one senator couldn't "make much of a change" anyway, Allie admitted. But she still saw a benefit to the action. Senator Cowan, Allie was convinced, would keep the students' need for more resources "there in her mind," so "it was a good strategy." And what Andy remembered most, months later? "She hugged us."

I have to admit, this meeting was probably the high point. The next two, the legislators were supportive, but they also seemed overcome to the point of inaction by the hold of powerful interests in state government.

❖

We couldn't pass something.

—Representative Michelle Reyes (IL-D)

Representative Michelle Reyes represents parts of west side Chicago and the near-west suburbs. Her district ranges from predominantly low-income to working class, and from Black and Latino to white—in mostly separate neighborhoods, given the segregation of the metro area. She is vice-chair of both the Latino Caucus and the education appropriations committee in the House. The bills she has sponsored show her to be a strong advocate for immigrant rights, undocumented students, and English learners.

When Representative Reyes comes to collect us from the waiting room, she apologizes for the broken air conditioner. It's a humid summer day, sweltering both inside and out. Aides pass around cold water and disappear discreetly.

Representative Reyes welcomes the Metro students by saying she was "really touched" by the letters they sent her, and she invites them to elaborate on what they've witnessed. She murmurs affirmation after each student's story. And when everyone has taken a turn, she tells them straight up, "It is unequal." She says that among her legislative allies, "We're trying to bring more equity, but we are not there. The problem right now is just trying to fund our schools. And that's been exhausting." Rather than talking about how to promote equity, the education committee has been focused on what to cut in an environment of declining revenue. "Sometimes I walk away from meetings" on the budget "with a knot in my stomach. My stomach hurts remembering that these are lives."

Knowing that school funding is so consequential, Representative Reyes wholeheartedly agrees "the way it's done right now is the wrong way to do it." But she sees little possibility of change on the horizon. "We don't have the money" to create true equity and "we don't have the whole body to support that" in the state legislature. "It's disheartening," she says, sounding disheartened herself, "but we couldn't pass something" that would truly reform the system. "I'm sorry, I don't have an answer for you," she concedes. "I don't see anything soon coming up for more equal funding distribution."

She does offer one tiny glimmer, and it's the Metropolitan Community Project itself. "This is where the public comes in. Young people who feel strongly and get involved. My encouragement to you is to keep challenging and engaging. The exchange you're doing is wonderful."

And "you know," she says, gesturing at the Metro students around the table, "this is what needs to occur in the state legislature. Seeing and feeling what the problem is. We are so removed from what you have witnessed." Thinking especially about the resistance of rural and suburban legislators to overhauling school funding, she imagines an exchange among "our colleagues" where they visit each other's districts and see resource inequalities up close. "We should try to connect because that leads to sensitivity and understanding. And that will make our decision-making more sensitive," she says. The metropolitan-ness of the project—city and suburban students together, advocating for change—appears to set a good example.

The students debrief.

Standing on the sidewalk before going home, the Taylor contingent does a brief recap. Jerry calls Representative Reyes "open-minded," Slim uses the word "supportive," and Bianca feels "she wanted our ideas on what could be done."

But the representative's sense of defeat was palpable. "She made it sound almost impossible," Slim said, repeating "almost impossible," for emphasis. Jerry definitely found her, "not hopeful." Perhaps the representative was a little trapped by her pessimism, Bianca said. "She's kind of in the middle. I think we should follow up with her and push her a little bit," to move her from being passively in favor to actively supporting.

The Metro students also react to something else that happened in the meeting: Representative Reyes repeatedly saying she needed to explain school funding "in simpler terms" so their "young minds" could grasp it. School funding policy *is* complicated, but the way she communicated with them felt off-putting, "like we were little kids," Bianca said. This was especially affronting given they'd worked hard to understand the issue. Mr. Ryan, who is used to explaining concepts to high school students, wished "she'd just given it to us straight. If we had questions, we could always ask them." These are some of the hazards when young people advocate for change.

The defeatism continues in the meeting with Representative Ed Miske, who sees a legislature immobilized by wealth and power.

❖

I don't see much opportunity to get something done.
—Representative Ed Miske (IL-D)

Representative Miske is known as a political operative. He's been in the House for decades, rising to deputy majority leader, and has a hard-nosed reputation. Mr. Bartel, who's interacted with him before on teacher union issues, warns the students before we go inside that Representative Miske will likely be gruff and all-business. The district office is in a diverse middle-class suburb just north of Chicago, not quite as prosperous as the one where Wyndham is located. The district also covers a few immigrant and working class neighborhoods on the city's northside.

"What can I do for you?" Representative Miske asks unsmilingly, once we're seated around the table. He does seem intimidating. But when the Metro students explain why they're there and what they want changed, he quickly establishes himself as a supporter. "My view is we should get off property taxes to pay for schools," he says frankly. "Then there will be more equitable funding." He spends the rest of the meeting, however, describing why that can't happen.

The thing about the current system is that wealthy communities get schools that are "the best they can be" and "those parents are not going to watch that be dismantled," he says. Any reform that is suggested, especially if it involves local money being re-routed to high-needs schools, will be opposed. Some parents may be "selfish," and some may be "fearful," but whatever their motivations, "they will think it's a risk to share the wealth in the education system." As soon as those parents are triggered, they will immediately get on the phone with their state representatives and try to shut the reform down.

And their representatives will listen. "In my line of work, the loudest and the squeakiest wheels get heard" because, and this is a simple political equation, "legislators want to be re-elected." This objective leads them to vote the way the "squeakier," more well-off families want.

And so, we get stuck: the status quo is protected by wealthy constituents and legislators doing what it takes to hold on to power. In combination with Republican and downstate opposition, "we don't have everyone we need," in the state legislature, "to pass something," Representative Miske says. Regretfully, he tells the students, "I don't see much opportunity to get something done."

This is obviously not good enough for the Metro students. "Something *has* to be done," Janelle tells him. "So how can we get all of the legislators to agree that public education is a major important issue? What are your ideas for us?"

Representative Miske says the Metro students are on the right track, but they need to go bigger. "Network with other people, meet all over the state," he says. "Get more schools and more students involved; get your neighbors and your cousins." He's putting the work on them but saying that's how the political process works. If the "have-nots" are not mobilized, he says, the legislature will remain a government of "the haves."

Because mostly what he sees is "each community fending for themselves," he tells the Metro students that their cross-community advocacy "makes an important point." Legislators normally define themselves narrowly as representing only their districts. "But," Representative Miske says slowly, as if it's dawning on him right then, "Our title is *State* Legislator. We may be elected in a given area but our responsibility is to the whole state—to everyone, every student, every parent."

I'm wondering now if this is the true heart of students' advocacy: reminding and pushing legislators to broaden their sense of responsibility.

The students debrief.

As Metro facilitators, we maybe overreacted in our warnings, since the first thing the students say afterwards is that Representative Miske wasn't that scary. "He wasn't aggressive" and "he wasn't mean" Janelle and Laila tell me, revealing their worries going into the meeting. Instead, the Metro students describe him as "really nice," "open-minded," and "almost grandfatherly."

The 'nothing can be done' sermon felt refreshingly "honest" to Jerry from Taylor, since it clarified what they were up against. Janelle appreciated that "he gave us ideas on how to make progress," ideas like, Jerry recapped, "we need to get more support to it, especially from downstate." At least Representative Miske was "supportive," Slim said, "and he knows for sure it can be done" even if change might not be quick or easy.

It's remarkable really, how these Taylor students take in bad news, how they turn it around into something hopeful.

Dear Legislator,
Hi! My name is Elizabeth I am
currently a Junior at Wyndham High school,
and I have been lucky enough to attend
some of the best schools this country's
public education system has to offer. This
year I have become involved with a program
at my school that facilitates an exchange
between Wyndham and Taylor High
school. Taylor High School is filled with
some amazing people that I have had the
pleasure to get to know over the course of
this past year and these are kids who
deserve the same opportunities I have
been given throughout my school career.
At the beginning of the year, we toured
each other's schools and what stood out
to me the most is the lack of human
resources. At Wyndham we have a whole
department of social workers, a whole department
of college counselors, a staff of nurses, and all
of these resources have impacted my high
school experience greatly. Taylor only
has one college counselor, and one part time
nurse. And while these might just be
minor problems in a system that is riddled
with problem, all these things add up to a
distinct gap between the different schools and
they give the kids at Taylor a lack
of opportunity. these differences
lead to a very big problem in our society,

this lack of education sets people up for failure when our school system is suspossed to be setting kids up for a successful future. I have been priveleged enough to have a fantastic education in the public school system and I hope one day that that quality of education is available to everyone. Thank you for your time.

Elizabeth

The summer comes to an end, and there are still two senators on the list who've responded to the students' letters. They are hours away, in the far north suburbs, but by chance they represent neighboring districts. So when an aide to one senator calls, I ask if she can help us meet jointly with the senator next door. There is much matching of schedules, but we finally manage to set a date for the late fall. For the first time, we will be meeting with a Republican and a Democrat, together.

❖

You're the answer.

—Senator Vanessa Schneider (IL-R) & Senator Laurie Irving (IL-D)

Because the meeting will be during a school day, every student in Metro can take part in the action. To make sure they get words in edgewise, we create an intentionally interactive format modeled after our smaller meetings. The agenda, which we send the senators rather than the other way around, is to explain the project, testify about the meaning of school resources, discuss possibilities for change, and reflect on educational equity. Sign-ups to speak publicly are open to any student who wants to. We take a preparatory field trip before the big day, so they can begin to organize their thoughts, questions, and reflections. The morning of, in their separate schools, the students write out what they want to say, to help them feel more confident when the moment comes.

On the Chicago bus, heading north out of the city, I overhear Mr. Ryan tell his students: "This is an opportunity to speak truth to power, and I hope you take advantage of it."

Senator Vanessa Schneider, the Republican, is a former special education teacher and small-town mayor. She represents a number of predominantly white and affluent suburbs in a more conservative part of northern Illinois. Many of the education-related bills she has co-sponsored in the Senate are measures to increase law enforcement's presence in schools, but she has also paid attention to needs of students with disabilities, given her prior career, and lent her support to the creation of the new task force on school funding.

Senator Laurie Irving, the Democrat in the neighboring district, represents towns that are more diverse, with sizable Latino and smaller Black populations, and several communities that are mostly white. Her district is also more liberal and middle class than her neighbor's. She's a former teacher union president, and she's joined her Democratic colleagues in proposals to change the tax structure in Illinois, increase the education budget, and make the distribution of funds more equal—bills that so far haven't passed.

The space the congressional aides arranged for us is a large union hall. The students sit in rows, at small narrow tables, mixed up by school. The senators sit together in front, facing the students, on a slightly raised dais. Senator Irving looks out on the crowd and says, "Before we get started, if you haven't talked to your state reps before, don't be nervous. We're here to learn from you."

Lucy courageously goes first, introducing herself and saying she attends Taylor. The senators ask her to stand so they can hear her, and after that, all of the Metro students stand to speak. Lucy continues, having volunteered to explain the Metropolitan Community Project:

> What we do on this project is we exchange: we do a community exchange and a school exchange, where we look at the similarities and differences. What we saw at Taylor and Wyndham in this project, we see the differences. We're both community schools, but we saw the schools are not being funded or treated equally.

We traveled on separate school buses, and the Taylor and Wyndham students didn't coordinate ahead of time who would speak when. But after Lucy opens, they instinctively take turns, creating vivid comparisons.

A really poignant moment comes when Elizabeth and Anna tag-team. At Wyndham, Elizabeth shares,

> My sophomore year, I had surgery, and I was out of school for a month. I had tutors come to my house. When I came back to school, we have a program where teachers help you at lunch and your free periods, to help you catch up. That completely saved me.

Anna's hand shoots up. I know for certain that she didn't plan to share this: it wasn't on her prep paper and she didn't bring it up at Taylor that morning. But she urgently wants to share something similar, and something wholly different:

> I also had surgery, and I was out for three months. We didn't have tutors, and nobody caught me up. When I came back, my teachers gave me a pack of work. I was trying to catch up, and I was able to. Except: I ended up failing one class. I didn't know how to do the work. I was trying to figure it out myself, and there was no one there to help.

Senator Irving, shakes her head and asks Elizabeth, amazed, "You literally had tutors come to your house?!" When Elizabeth affirms this, Senator Schneider turns to Anna and asks how falling behind "affected you emotionally." They seem to be absorbing the effect of so much disparity.

After more Metro students give their testimony, Senator Irving exclaims in exasperation, "This is not working, folks!" Senator Schneider thinks what she's hearing is "unfair," too. "Thank God you recognize the fact that this is discriminatory." That's the Republican speaking.

The testimony from the suburbs appears to make a particularly strong impression. When Sarah suggests that with all their extra funding, "I think we could give some of that money to Taylor and still be strong enough," Senator Schneider gives her compliments. "I think it's great for you to say you will take a little less, to give someone who gets substantially less something more. We need you." It's true, Senator Irving says, appreciatively. "We don't have enough people who say that. I look at those at Wyndham, I look at your courage, and I go . . ." Just then, she actually starts clapping.

Something about the senators' reaction catches while I'm listening. It is wonderful that the Wyndham students are here, advocating alongside their peers in the city. But the attention and kudos are going to youth who already have so much. Applause and compliments for the Taylor students, meanwhile, seem to go missing. It is almost as if the senators believe it is easy for the Chicago students to say, since they're the ones in need, and they're the ones who will be the direct recipients of any change.

But we know it's not easy, after hearing before how vulnerable the Taylor students feel, how scared they are that others will judge them in the way city youth are almost always judged. When Janelle states that, with limited guidance counseling, "a lot of students at Taylor don't know what to do with themselves," that takes strength to admit. It is brave when Angelica presses for greater college support, revealing how a low score on an AP exam makes her worry about the future.

Asked by Senator Schneider about "poverty issues," Ailany could withdraw; this is after all a discomfort-inducing label, a step away from possible stereotype. Instead, Ailany goes personal. "My mother starts work at 5:30 in the morning and she doesn't get home until 6:30 at night," she says. "Our parents push themselves to work a lot to help their kids. That means they can't help as much with school."

These are all hard, courageous things to say, things that can leave them open to prejudice. But they say them anyway, for the purpose of pushing these influential decision-makers for a fairer educational system. I don't think the senators see this, but we can acknowledge it, knowing what we know, after spending more time with the Taylor kids.

Something I don't think the students are aware of, but you can see from the outside if you are more familiar with the debate, is they are being pulled into controversies over school funding, like: Does money matter? Is it the amount of money or how money is spent? Shouldn't hard work conquer all?

Almost as soon as the students begin testifying, the challenges start coming. The senators ask multiple times, "Do the differences come down to money?" in a tone suggesting that it's possible they don't.

Later, we hear another theory: Senator Schneider asks, "Is it the students who are different? Or is it bricks and mortar?" Sarah, who's from the suburbs, jumps in for support: "The Wyndham and the Taylor students have the same goals. It's just the educational system is holding people back from putting those goals into reality." I don't even know if she knows what 'bricks and mortar' means, but she definitely isn't letting the city students bear this burden.

Still, Senator Irving feels compelled to tell them, "Education is important. You can have a fabulous education, and if you do not work, you are not going to be successful." Of course that's true, and the Metro students are there because they understand the importance of education. But the students are also trying to say: if your education is constricted, you have fewer chances to be successful, even when you are working hard.

The senators differ on the best fix, given their political persuasions. The hurdle to getting equal funding in Illinois, Senator Irving argues, is "how do we find the money?" But Senator Schneider retorts, "I'm going to disagree there. It's not the amount of money. It's the allocation of funds," a matter of having the right "priorities." Ben, a student from Taylor, observes later, "I think they were low-key arguing with each other."

They are, somewhat. But even as Senator Irving supports greater funding, she pushes the Metro students to prioritize. In her "perfect world," every student would have the "same opportunity," but it is "more realistic," she says, "to ask: What are the things that are most important? Is it services? Is it variety of classes? Is it a focus on college? We need to decide." Senator Schneider suggests it is early childhood education, which does little for the kids sitting in front of her, who are already in high school.

The Metro students, of course, are telling them it is all of these things. It reminds me of something Jonathan Kozol wrote way back when in *Savage Inequalities*: how the children in wealthy areas aren't being asked to choose (1991, p. 79). Wyndham is a college-preparatory school, while also offering every class one can imagine, and a whole spectrum of services. No one is asking the suburban students to "be realistic" about their education.

Unexpectedly, Senator Schneider leaves early. She apologizes several times before she departs, telling the students that her staff double-booked her, and she has another event in the community to attend. This is a simple, maybe understandable, mix-up; the students will remember it later.

Afterwards, the Metro students press the senator who remains on what she is willing to do. Senator Irving names the solution she supports, what's called "needs-based funding:" giving schools serving language learners, low-income students, and students with disabilities greater funds. "We need more money in areas of poverty, not less," she argues. She understands there will be resistance to the idea, but she rhetorically asks the holdouts, the "wealthier people:" "Why wouldn't you want to help other people in this state have a quality education?"

That's where the Metro students come in, she says. They can help convince reluctant parents, and opponents in the legislature, that change is needed. "You'd think it would be simple, a no-brainer. But grownups are complex. I think you're the answer: students who are willing to come testify." Their experiences, their witnessing of inequality first-hand, are affecting "data," she says. "Like manna from heaven."

So she makes them a promise: "That's one thing I could do, is get you to Springfield," the state capitol. It's a long way, a four-hour trip, but Senator Irving commits her office's resources. "We could fund a bus," she says. The students will remember this, too.

The forum ends in a kind of crescendo. The Metro students argue passionately for educational equality. Like Rusty, from Chicago, who stands and says, "We all deserve an equal opportunity. It's not fair" that "wealthy" students receive "a wide range" while students who "aren't fortunate" are given "not enough." Riding this wave, Senator Irving closes with a shout, "I have one question for all of you as you are continuing this work: Why aren't you all suing the state?! What about a class action lawsuit? Why aren't you demanding equality? Why aren't you asking the question: why isn't her education as good as hers?"

There is tumult and excitement in the room as she says this. Everyone gets up, and the students swarm her, talking animatedly. Alex, rushing by the Taylor teacher, yells to him, "We're going to sue, Mr. Ryan!"

When it's over, and we're coming out of the union hall, Lena points to the parking lot and laughs. There, side-by-side, is a shuttle emblazoned with Wyndham's logo and the rented (and dented) yellow school bus that will take the Taylor kids home. "The senators should've come out here with us and looked at these buses!," Lena exclaims, still laughing. "That shows the difference!"

The students debrief.

Back at Taylor, debriefing the day, the reaction is a swell of positivity. "I fell in love with Senator Irving," Rosa says breathlessly. Anna "liked" both senators, and she was particularly impressed by "how they interacted with us and asked us questions." Sensitive to feeling dismissed, Denise appreciat-

Gathering outside the state capitol. Photo courtesy of author.

ed how the senators "acknowledged the differences between our schools," which is basically the same as saying, 'they believed what we said.' To the Taylor students, that recognition communicated empathy for their struggles.

Most think Senator Irving can be counted on in her offer to help because she understands the necessity of change. "Sooner or later, she'll end up doing something for us," Rosa believes. "She seemed trustworthy," Slim says, "like she wouldn't go back on her word. She really was for equal education."

The Wyndham students think so too. "She was able to respond with such determination," Sarah says, that it became contagious. "We came out of the meeting energized," Adrianna tells me, of her suburban peers, "and ready to push harder." They are especially taken by the idea of suing for equal funding. Narrating the moment when that suggestion took hold, Adrianna recalls, "We were all packing up and she was like, 'hold on a second, why don't you sue the state?' That blew everyone away." In a good way, Sarah explains. "It was really motivating to hear people with such power telling us we should do something."

At school, the Wyndham students excitedly start planning. They have a feeling of forward momentum. "It seemed like we were going to get somewhere," Maggie says, looking back. "We were going to go to Springfield, and we were going to start a lawsuit." This mixture of idealism and faith; you want to hold onto it.

"I don't want to break anyone's hearts," Ben interjects, bringing us down to earth, "but I thought Irving was kind of BSing it. Like she said she was going to be busing us to Springfield. I don't think it's gonna happen." Janelle thinks Senator Irving was almost "too nice:" "people say a lot of things." She isn't sure she will help as much as she said. About the lawsuit idea, "when she was telling us to sue and get lawyers," Keke muses, "I think she was telling us stuff just to tell us." These kids are already cynical readers of politics, and it's interesting that they're all from Taylor. The track record of the city's politicians is not one of promises kept.

❖

Bipartisan Inaction

I don't want to break anyone's hearts either, but they were right, it didn't work out. We got caught in a struggle for power. When the Metro students met with Senator Irving, she was serving on a task force to revise school funding, which ultimately recommended the redistribution of some state monies to high-needs schools. The state board of education examined the proposed bill and released a detailed spreadsheet showing the gains and losses projected for each school district.

Suburban districts saw their share of state dollars drop the most. "We were hit hard," Senator Irving's aide told me. "The numbers were dramatic, more than we were expecting." The decreased funding makes sense, because these are the places with the most local revenue. But these are also the areas where wealth and influence combine, and they were not having it.

Op-eds and outrage at suburban public forums created an immense backlash against the reform, and even progressive lawmakers like Senator Irving backed away from the bill. At the same time, the legislature became consumed with the state budget and its deficits.

Amidst all of this, we had trouble getting our contacts back on the phone. No one told us we couldn't come, but the offer to pay for a bus, and to host us in Springfield, floated away.

The school funding bill, amazingly, passed in the Senate, but it died in the House without a vote being taken. That wasn't the final resting place—

with continued advocacy, and multiple rounds of revision, the bill came back to life in new form. But it took years to come to fruition, and the Metro students didn't know yet that there'd be light on the other side.

As for legal action, the suburban students had the connections to run with it, but they were stymied pretty quickly. "We all talked about starting a lawsuit, and I actually got involved," Sarah told me. "My mom's friend is a lawyer who used to work a lot with education, so I talked to her about it." What she discovered was there had been lawsuits before over school funding that "didn't work." According to the Center for Tax and Budget Accountability, an independent state watchdog, Illinois has "some of the weakest constitutional language in the country with regards to education." All of the previous attempts to sue over inequitable funding have failed as a result. Looking back at the meeting with Senator Irving, "she was giving us ideas, but the ideas weren't something we could follow through with," Sarah concluded. Sigh.

❖

Action Reflections

We got actual senators to sit down and listen to us.
—The Metro students

This is probably obvious: the Metro students were disappointed by these outcomes. The senators under-delivered, to put it mildly. "We needed to have the support, and it fell apart," Maggie from Wyndham told me. "I'm disappointed that it got pushed aside." Trina of Taylor recalled the trip was Senator Irving's idea in the first place. But then, "when it came to sending us to Springfield, she just disappeared." It was hard to square the senators' seeming support with this result. "The whole meeting was so powerful and exciting and, 'Yeah! We're going to change!'" Slim remembered feeling. "And then they didn't follow through. Now, I don't know." It was difficult to go from that high to this low.

Perhaps because they experienced this downswing, their judgment of Senator Schneider's early departure grew harsher in retrospect. "One of the senators left," Alex from Taylor recalled. With some sarcasm in his voice, he supposed it came down to their "*so-busy* schedules." Yet, "if they really cared about it, they would take the time to just listen to us for a couple of seconds," he said.

There was agreement over at Wyndham from Adrianna. "Schneider left after a short while. She was not willing to stay. Obviously, she had a different commitment. But still, it shows." What it showed, well, Adrianna left that dangling.

Looking back, this seemed to be a case of "more talk than action," said Xavia, because the senators didn't keep to their commitments. "I think they kind of fooled us," Trina said, into believing they'd do something. The legislators "looked really into it," Lena agreed. But she'd been warned. "A friend told me, never trust politicians, they always promise something and never do it." And, ultimately, in her view, that's what happened. "I noticed that this year."

Or perhaps, in Senator Irving's case, she really did want change, but "she was in a position where she can only push so hard, and then it's putting her in a less powerful place," Adrianna posited.

Either way, the Metro students guessed that the senators' political calculations did not include them in the equation, not really. They concluded the year with a little more distrust over politics than when they began.

On this note of cynicism, you might think they'd dismiss the whole experience in hindsight, questioning whether it was worth the effort to have engaged these two senators at all. That's not what happened. Across kids and schools, the Metro students called the meeting valuable, even fun, despite what happened next. Here's a cross-section of what I heard: "I really enjoyed it," "I liked it," "it was nice, very comfortable to talk to them," "it went well, the conversations we had were pretty strong," "that was pretty interesting," and "one of the best meetings we ever had."

Some of the most cynically disappointed students were also some of the proudest of their work. "I liked our plan of action," said Shana, despite her "wish it could've gone further." While Rusty called it "a bummer" they didn't visit the state capitol, and Trina especially worried she'd been misled, both students called their testimony that day "a great strategy." An early adopter of skepticism towards the senators' promises, Janelle still complimented the Metro group's action. "I thought it was a great move that we've done."

The move's value was that it felt real. "Even if it was a small step, it felt really good to be doing something instead of just talking about the issues," said Shana. These were bona fide decision-makers with power. "We got actual senators to sit down and listen to us and hear what we have to say," Trina said proudly. Disappointed as she was that the lawsuit idea fizzled, Sarah nonetheless sounded a little starstruck: "I was able to ask a state legislator about something, and she was so open to our ideas and questions." Not only that, "we had both sides," Slim recalled. "We had the Republican and the Democrat. And they both agreed," to the credit of the Metro students' testimony, "on how big of an injustice the funding is." This was ultimately the point: to advocate to an audience that could actually do something about inequity.

Angelica was pretty sure their message landed. "Its impact: they saw what we were going through, and they realized." Her wish that they'd "actually gone to Springfield," did not supplant her belief in this success. The authenticity of the experience mattered to the Metro students, whatever the outcome. They were not so fragile as to take setbacks as defeat.

❖

Advocating for equity with a state legislator. Photo courtesy of author.

School Funding Reform, at Last

What is the saying about the 'long arc of justice'? (King Jr., 1968) For Metro, it was long, but it eventually came closer. Almost four years later, with a different group of students, we finally went to Springfield on the cusp of a vote on the school funding bill, in its latest version.

Just before we left for our trip, the Metro students held a peace circle with two of the bill's co-sponsors, to bring them closer to the kids it would affect. We arrived at the state capitol in the middle of a debate over whether the state should direct more money to schools with higher needs.

Entering the rotunda, the Metro students carried signs they made themselves, with the sayings: "Educational Equity," "Our Teachers' Working Conditions Are Our Schools' Learning Conditions," and "Education Is Power." They met with a half-dozen legislators, outside the hearing room with voices echoing off the marble, and inside cramped offices with polished desks. They took turns sharing what they learned about their partner school, and its contrasts with their own; they pushed their representatives to close the gap.

Senator Dave Lewin, who'd been working on the reform for four years, said that word of the Metro coalition was spreading. "Senators and Representatives here know what you're doing. They know about your project," he said. A Republican co-sponsor, Representative Ron Griffiths, told them their testimony was factoring into the deliberations going on behind the scenes. "We're talking about you in our committee meetings," he told the students. "What you're doing here is making a difference."

Also that day, the local public radio station interviewed our students. The audio from the story aired in Springfield a few days later, during the continuing hearings on school funding, and then broadcast statewide. A full-length news article and a pictorial slideshow accompanied the radio story online. The story got picked up on TV. So the legislature heard from the Metro kids even when they were no longer there.

On the last day of the session, in a squeaker-could've-gone-either-way outcome, the school funding bill passed. The legislation redesigned the state's education funding formula, sending more to schools where low-income, multilingual, and special education students attend.

Advocating for equity with a state legislator. Photo courtesy of author.

With no votes to spare, all of the legislators the Metro students talked to over the project's history voted "yes" except for two neutral "presents." These included state officials who previously were not natural constituencies for school funding reform: suburban legislators, rural legislators, and Republicans.

New monies are now going to city schools, and anywhere else where there are a lot of students with greater obstacles to their success. It is not enough, it is not equal still, and public money went to private schools too for a time, as part of a concession to secure passage. The arc still needs bending. But what the reform law did was change the concept of how we resource schools in the state, making equity part of the equation. And the Metro students had something to do with pushing the margin of its success.

❖

Note

1. The Illinois state legislators' names in this book are pseudonyms. The details related to their districts, leadership positions, committee appointments, bill sponsorship, and voting records are real and have not been changed. When introduced, the state legislators are identified by their political party, "D" for Democrat and "R" for Republican.

References

King, M.L., Jr. (1968, March 31). *Remaining awake through a great revolution.* Speech given at the National Cathedral, Washington D.C. https://www.youtube.com/watch?v=DTEPRWyIyRA

Kozol, J. (1991). *Savage inequalities: Children in America's schools.* New York, NY: Crown.

Mosteller, F. (1995). The Tennessee study of class size in early school grades. *Critical Issues for Children and Youths,* 5(2): 113–127.

PART III CODA

The Ups and Downs of Student Activism

THE EDUCATIONAL SYSTEM CAN feel like an immovable force, a boulder that won't move. Pushing against it is really hard and in the moment it can seem like it's not budging. In Metro, on the shadow-side of the rock, policymakers reacted with dismissal or, maybe worse, empty promises. On the sunnier-side, the Metro students finally saw school funding shift.

The hard part first: Not all of the legislators felt it. The students shared their distress over missing things they needed, and their embarrassment over having more than enough, but it didn't always connect. With some lawmakers, there was little reaction to the feeling and the experience behind students' words. Filling in that blank was what looked like coldness or disbelief, as if the students didn't know their own lives. These legislators pushed out other explanations—it probably wasn't inequity, they said. It was the size of the school, the misadministration of funds, or the lack of priorities. There were probably other fixes too, they suggested: like choosing resources wisely, helping littler kids, or simply working hard and acting right. And if there wasn't a problem, and schools and students could work with what they had, then there was little for a legislator to do. In these cases, there seemed to be a washing of hands.

And then there were the meetings where the legislators said they believed, that they truly supported the students and wanted to do something. But alas, they couldn't: there was no money; there was a pension crisis; the political opposition was too strong. Some of the most powerful decision-makers in the state seemed to be claiming, 'we don't have the power.' What we were hearing, the Taylor teacher Mr. Ryan noticed, was a "subtext of hopelessness." This defeatism sounded genuine, as if the legislators really thought they were trapped. But it also protected them, providing the cover to say, in a frustratingly passive voice, 'there's nothing to be done.' Even if they had the vote count right, something about this feels like evasion. If not them, who?

We can add to this list the most obvious disappointment, that there were legislators who committed but didn't follow through. I don't know if they know how much small reversals—leaving early, not providing a bus—contribute to an erosion of faith, a deflation of participatory enthusiasm. That has to cost more than a ride to the state capitol or lateness to the next event, but I'm not sure the legislators are weighing it this way. The Metro students, as I said, aren't fragile, but their political engagement is young. There is a caretaking that's needed here, to preserve and grow what the legislators found so striking: the unitedness of city and suburban kids around educational equality.

Turning to the brighter side, many of the legislators were touched by the nearness and pain of educational longing. They seemed moved, like they were connecting to the city students' testimony on an emotional level. It's common to say, 'you can't look into someone's heart,' and of course, we can't. But the Metro students saw them up close and seemed inclined to believe their expressions of care. So the original goal, of getting to legislators "on a human level," seemed to work—for many. There is a chance that this inner effect, the feeling evoked when students told them of their shock and hurt over resources denied, seeped into the decisions they made. Even if the power-broking overrode it, an additional hurdle needed to be cleared, the gut reaction suppressed. Or maybe that feeling was listened to and acted on.

To adults, the fact that we fund schools based on what communities are able to pay has settled into reality. The Metro students have no such jadedness—they think it's outrageous. In asking how school funding could possibly work this way, they de-naturalized the way we do things (Freire, 1998, 2006). And that's something: to get legislators to go through the process of explaining why an unfair system shelters in place. The officials were forced to go deeper, which eventually led them to concede the role of wealth in politics. It's an obvious confession, but one that needs to be said out loud: 'in state government, the very institution we belong to, some have more say.'

Given this pattern, the legislators admitted they were impressed by the participation of the suburban students in Metro. It was strange but refreshing to them to see the younger versions of residents who call their offices and contribute to their campaigns acting beyond a status-quo self-interest. The presence of advantaged kids in a coalition for equity drew the representatives' attention. While this is a sad commentary on the gravitation of wealth and whiteness, it is, potentially, a model of privilege being harnessed for a social good.

The Metro students held up a kind of mirror to the state legislators. They were teenagers, but they'd joined up across geography, income, race, and school. What excuse did the legislature have, then, for its own fractures and disunities, for caring about only the narrowest slice? The togetherness of the students in front of them prodded several legislators to take a state-wide view of their responsibilities.

Some lawmakers brought the state-wide view to work. They shared the students' testimony on the Senate floor and in deliberations with colleagues. They met with the Metro members when we visited the state capitol, some voluntarily and some after being intercepted in the lobby by tenacious high school students. The votes shifted slowly to the "yes" column for a law that now sends more funds to schools where low-income, multilingual, and special education students attend.

Overall, the Metro students received both backing and brushoffs for their activism. The ups and downs caused some cynicism about the genuineness of state leaders and extended their estimates (correctly) of how long it would take for change to materialize. Across students and schools though, the Metro students felt pride and joy in their campaigns, even knowing there was more work ahead.

❖

References

Freire, P. (1998). *Pedagogy of freedom: Ethics, democracy, and civic courage*. Lanham, MD: Rowman & Littlefield.

Freire, P. (2006). *Pedagogy of the oppressed* (30th anniversary ed.). New York, NY: Continuum.

PART IV

Metro Student Outcomes

INTRODUCTION

THIS SECTION TRIES TO answer the most frequently asked question: How did the project affect the kids? The Taylor and Wyndham students, as you know by now, began the project in very different places. This means their take-aways are different too. We'll go to each school in these chapters, just like I did when I went to interview the Metro students for the last time. It's summer, so you'll need a sweater for the air conditioning at Wyndham. At Taylor, prepare to be as hot as the kids. In both places you'll recognize that buzzy, end-of-the-year feeling in the hallways.

CHAPTER SIX

Personal Change: The Taylor Students

WE'RE LIVING IN A time of division and backlash, but there are hopeful actions happening too: police accountability protests, unionization drives, Out of the Shadows celebrations, and many local efforts that don't make the news. These movements share intersecting goals of systemic change in law enforcement, labor practices, and immigration policy. The public educational system, with its underlying inequalities, is overdue for a similar reckoning. The question is, how do we build that movement? How, especially, can the youth most harmed—Black students, Latino students, low-income students, immigrant students, in all the ways they overlap—claim their power to transform the system? A Metro-style alliance may be a route to this goal, with many imperfections to work out along the way.

In order to change the system, people first need to see it. In this case, we're talking about truly being able to see the extreme disparity across public schools in our country. But it is intentionally hidden, cloaked in a false merit narrative—that people who are "smarter" or work harder earn high-opportunity schools. The high school curriculum doesn't demystify this very much: Civics classes rarely cover the state and federal role in education, or how school funding works. Our splintered living arrangements also make it hard to see. Well-funded schools tend to be in separate places, outside the action of low-income youth's lives.

Developing a Wider View

Many, many people over the years have suggested to me, either outright or by the tone of their voices, that it is probably cruel to show city kids such a wealthy suburban school. I understand the concern, and it's something we've talked about often in the project, that we show them the school with purpose and care and that we support their processing of an upsetting reality. It seemed fitting to ask the Taylor students the question directly: Why did you want to see that school? What did you get from seeing it?

So first, here's what they said it would be like without this experience, if they'd stayed in place. "There's so much more than just the walls of your school," Janelle told me. "If you don't know what's outside the world, then you're just going to be trapped in a box, and we don't need that no more." Angelica used a similar metaphor: knowing about the suburban school is important so "you're not just stuck in your school, like, 'Oh, this is it.' You're exploring other things." And Lena described her own, formerly in-the-box thinking. "I wish I could've done it earlier," she said, speaking of Metro. "Because I was so close-minded, like, we're all in this little world."

What the Taylor students are describing is a world hemmed in by an unequal society. I'm thinking of this in combination with other parts of their life story they've told me about over the years. How few of the students or their parents can afford cars to get around. How undocumented families with cars take back roads rather than highways, spending hours longer on the road on infrequent trips, to avoid being pulled over. How Taylor parents, concerned about the safety of the train, often don't let their kids use it. How many of the Taylor kids have never traveled out-of-state, except for some who've visited family in Mexico. How the kids avoid walking down certain streets, and being on certain blocks, for their protection. How they often go straight home and indoors after school, for the same reason, or to take care of younger siblings. How, during a project field trip to a gentrifying part of the neighborhood only ten minutes from school, it was many of the Taylor students' first time there. The area is "catering to the middle-class-upper-class population," noted Ms. Sofia, a local organizer, and "hasn't done a lot of work" to be "open to all types of people in the community." And perhaps the biggest one where Metro is concerned: how before it began, just about every Taylor student told me they'd never been to any suburb ever.

This is not to say that the Taylor kids do not have in-depth knowledge of the community and school they are in. Rusty told me she felt "lucky" to live where she does, because the suburban students "don't know the outside world really, like how hard it actually is. They get everything handed to them." She's deservedly proud of this knowledge—many more people deal with hardship than prosperity, and it's an expertise to understand struggle, and resilience. And Rusty is about right on Wyndham's score too: they don't know much about this. Lena noticed the same thing, when she took her Wyndham group-mates on a tour of her school. "I would tell them, 'How is it possible that them, being a public high school, didn't know what was going on with other public high schools in urban areas?'" She knew all about it: the resource obstacles in her way, the effort she made to do well in school anyway. Allie thought it would be good "if you put a Wyndham kid here for a day, they would see what we go through. They would see a totally different world for us than it is for them."

These judgments are all pretty fair. The Taylor students are savvier about what life can throw at you; they seem hardier about handling it, too. The suburban students are sheltered, and they don't know much about life in the city beyond the tourist version: downtown, baseball games, and outdoor summer concerts. It does seem like a different world.

But wealthy suburban communities are part of the "real world" too. To know them is to know what is available to the advantaged in our society, to upper-income people and white people (who are often the same people). So we can take the Taylor kids' truths and look at them in reverse, right? That Taylor students aren't very familiar with the ease of privilege, and what it provides. That Taylor students don't know a lot about suburban public schools, although they go to a public school themselves. That if they went to Wyndham for a day, they'd see what suburban kids "go through": a seemingly different world, a passageway to power in society.

The Taylor students had only a hazy idea of what that part of the world looked like. "I didn't know, I didn't *really* know," Slim said, of her time before Metro and visiting the suburbs. "I didn't hear of the school before," or really of any school quite like that. So there were "things I didn't see." It's not that they knew nothing of disparity; they just didn't see how far it went. "Before I was in this project," Mia told me, "I knew there was a difference, but I didn't know to what extent. It's something that's not drawn to you," in your everyday life, in your everyday education. Lena assumed she had some approximation of the distance between her education and the suburbs, expecting it to be "just a little bit." Reflecting on her underestimate, she told me, "This is the first year I've done this, and I never knew about this. I didn't know it was a huge difference."

Of course, you could study the issue in class—read a textbook or see a video. Or you could watch almost any high school drama on TV, with their lavish suburban locales. But the Taylor students said they needed to actually be in the space. "Since we don't see it and don't live it every day, it's important to actually get the experience, and the stories, from the students who do," Bianca told me. "So we have a better understanding." And unlike book learning, or "all talk," Angelica said, by being there, "you know it for yourself, and you get to know the real situation."

When the Taylor students describe what visiting Wyndham meant to them, it's like they're zooming out from their immediate surroundings. "Now that I saw everything," Lena told me, "I'm so open-minded. I'm like, 'Wait a minute!'" The critical piece, Lena said, was "when you see other schools, and other students, you notice a huge difference. You notice there are things going on out there, in the world." In a way, the city students were too close to it before, dealing with injustice on a daily basis but not seeing it clearly for what it was, or where it came from. The wider view showed them something they needed to know about inequality. "I think it's good to know," Xavia told me, what it's like "over there, the way it's set up, and the system." To go "over there" is to understand the world, and the educational system, more fully.

When I asked the Taylor Metro students what they took from this experience, it was a lesson on inequality. "I learned," Slim told me, "how unfair the system was. It opened my eyes." This was their most frequently mentioned outcome from participating in Metro, this big reveal. "I learned," Angelica responded, "well, it opened my eyes to an injustice. Like, I didn't know there was an injustice, but I realized." The abundance on display at the suburban high school—there was just so much more—pushed this realization. "Knowing what I can be offered at Wyndham, it's like I see the unfairness," Janelle reacted.

I am not saying, though, that learning this wasn't hard. Xavia, you might remember, said these lessons "put me down." Lucy punctuated her discussion of Wyndham with, "What the hell?!" Lena felt "mixed emotions: I'm so happy to learn this experience, but then again, it's so sad how it's so unfair." It was upsetting to witness the cornucopian education in suburbia, but the

Taylor kids said they wouldn't go back. "It's important to know because it's not fair that they have more privileges than us," Anna told me. She's right: it's not fair. That's why we're doing this. "We should be able to receive the same privileges, the same education."

Recognizing Limits and Strengths

Before they were jolted by this comparison, when Taylor was mostly what they knew, how they were being educated, and what they were being provided, didn't provoke a lot of scrutiny. "I never really thought about it," Trina shared. "I was just like, 'Oh, I'm in school, I'm in school.'" School was just, well, school. "We're so used to having this, we think it's normal," was Ailany's mindset. Up to this point, the world around them seemed to confirm this normalcy. "I went through grade school, and I had this school that was just like Taylor, it was low-funded and everything," Eddy told me. "I just thought that's how it was. Same thing with middle school," he continued, "thought that's how it was. I had friends go to other schools, and they basically had the same thing, so I thought that's how education was." Constraint at Taylor just became part of the natural landscape.

Coming back to their school, after seeing the suburban one, changed how they saw it. "It opens my eyes of what school I actually go to," said Rusty. "Now I see more. Then, I didn't," said Slim, of her altered state. "It changed my mind forever about public school, about any school, about education period." A little unexpectedly, Lucy discovered, "even though I'm here as a student, there's things I didn't know about my school, and I learned through these field trips."

Going there and coming back made certain things stand out more. "I feel like, you don't know what you're missing out of until you actually know what's out there," Mia told me. It's hard to see an absence until you know what's present somewhere else. It was helpful, they said, to see their school in this kind of relief. "Knowing what they're being offered makes me think about what I should be offered," Janelle said. "Because I see my limits here at Taylor," after being in the suburbs. In her indefatigable way, Janelle added, "I'm not letting that stop me, of course." But the contrast did make what was missing feel tangible, recognized as a real need. "I thought schools were just like that," Eddy said. "I didn't realize it was because we don't have what everybody else has." And then Metro came along and showed him what was being left out.

Once they saw what well-funded schools had, having less was no longer something to just endure. "We think that's the norm, that that's regular when it comes to schools, and that shouldn't be the case," Eddy argued. This was their big turnaround, to stop seeing the limits being placed on their school as normal (Freire, 2006). It took the shock of comparison, Mia said, "to see that it's really not fair, what we don't have." While she'd become expert at maneuvering around the gaps, it occurred to Lucy that they shouldn't be there in the first place. As one example, "we have to deal with the fact that our library is closed—but it shouldn't be like that," she decided. "And," she added, "it's good to see other schools and see how it's not like that" to verify, "we shouldn't be dealing with that." Making do with less could not continue to be the regular price of going to school.

I know this sounds dangerous, to have the Taylor kids coming back to their school wanting more. I know you're worried they'll feel bad. But it doesn't sound like dejection or disappointment to me. It sounds like an assertion of rights. "Knowing about Wyndham's education helps me know what I deserve," Janelle declared. Not just her, though. The entire student body: "We deserve more."

While "unfair" was the watchword when they saw the suburban school, "deserve," was the sentiment when they came home to theirs. I heard it over and over at the end of the school year. Once Trina participated, "I realized that there is a better education for everyone and that we do deserve an equal opportunity." When Rusty went to the suburbs and saw that school, "It's like, I see how other people have it better, and I feel I deserve better." Walking alongside Elizabeth on the tour of Wyndham, Lucy's reaction was, "I deserve her education." What was the basis for this feeling, that they're worthy of every resource seen at the suburban school? "We are humans as well as them," Lena says, as if explaining the obvious (which she is). "We deserve the equal rights." Her confidence relies on the most basic moral values. And because I'm still asking questions, she moves to shut this down for good. "We should get the equality. That's it." If we take city students' humanity as a given, what's left to understand? That's it.

By comparing educations, the Taylor students also learned more about what they had: a close-knit, against-adversity school. Perhaps out of necessity, the ethos of Taylor was not so individually-focused and competitive. "I feel like living for others is more enjoyable and more spiritual," Ailany said, and these values were supported all around her. They didn't have things on as grand a scale as Wyndham, but they had community, connection, and passion, and these bring life meaning. "They do get better stuff than us, that's true," Papi admitted, of the school out there in the suburbs. "But we have some things they don't have: We have art that makes things rich and shows the personal view. We Latinos stick together. We talk in the hallways but we still get to classes on time." The personal view continued in class. Anna suddenly appreciated how, "Our teachers, they're doing what they can for us, with our low budgets and everything. They really try to help us out. I wasn't realizing it until I joined the program." The Taylor environment could be challenging but it was met by teachers and students with mutual help and care. Coming back from the suburban school made Taylor's connective tissue more visible.

Developing Activists

What perils are there for a system when kids see it for what it is? "When we know about other schools, we're like, 'There has to be a change in the world. It's not ok for this to happen,'" Ailany argues. "So we're more informed, and we're able to do something about it, rather than just thinking, 'This is what we have and all there is to it.'"

Since taking action is built-in to Metro, the city students' participation helped propel them towards change. "I learned that we should fight for what we want," Lali told me, after Metro ended for the year. "How did that happen?," I asked. "Because we *are* fighting for something," Lali replied. "We are together, two schools, fighting for something we want. We're fighting for equal education."

And they sound stronger from the experience, like they found the power to push back. "It made me feel like I could actually do something," Angelica said. "Like I was helping the school. Because I stood up for what I believe." It sounds a little like a tautology, but engaging in action made them feel like activists.

The Taylor kids each had someone specific in mind whom they were making change for—and it was not themselves. Without my asking, they brought their relatives, classmates, and friends into the conversation. For Alex, it was his siblings. "A better foundation for the school, that's what I'm hoping for," he said. "That's what this project is all about. I got two little sisters that come here. I want them to be successful." Bianca explained it was her extended family: "I'm bummed and bothered by how we fund schools. I want to do something about it. I'm thinking about my nephews and nieces, and what's best for them." For other Taylor students, it was "the youth that's coming up," through their high school, who felt like family even if they weren't technically related. Eddy told me, "Even though this is my last year, I want to make it better, I want to fix it. That way, other kids can have the opportunities to do what I wanted to do here." Their change-focus was all-inclusive, extending to their friends, family, and neighbors.

To get there, they became ambassadors for the cause, stopping classmates in the halls and bringing it up after school. The list of people they talked to about Metro was long: friends, cousins, their mom, an uncle's friend, their dad, 'my sister,' 'my brother'. "I'm always telling my family about all these issues, and they don't realize it until I tell them," Rusty said. "I talked to a lot of my friends from school, even at work, and they were shocked," Lucy relayed. "I was like, 'in my personal view, the way they're dividing the money, it's just unfair.'"

The response solidified their identities as change-makers. A somewhat reserved student, Moe told me his family was "really surprised I was getting involved" with educational inequity, because normally, "they don't see me as a guy who likes to fight for other people." He claimed the role for himself now. "I am" that kind of person, he said. Slim encountered a similar double-take, even though, inside Metro, she looked like a natural. "They were surprised," she said, speaking of her relatives. But in a good way. Her "family members were like, 'It's a good thing you're doing. It's something really good for everybody.'" Within Janelle's family, "My mom and dad are very proud. They see what I'm doing, and they're like, 'She's doing it for a good cause.'" Trina had her mom's full support. "She told me she really likes that I'm doing this because she understands how I feel. She wishes that no matter where she lived, her child had the same, equal education." That Trina and the other Taylor students were working to fulfill this wish was acknowledged with pride. It was affirming for the Taylor students to receive this—you can tell from the warmth in their voices. Their families saw them in a new light, so they saw themselves that way, too.

Waiting for the bus near Taylor High. Photo courtesy of author.

Developing Solidarity

The Taylor students also felt affirmed by the support they received from outside their community, from the suburban students. "They see the inequality," Lucy said of the Wyndham students, "and they tried to see our struggles being a student at Taylor." For the Taylor kids, the project did something simple but powerful: their daily efforts to make do in an under-resourced school felt seen. This was something different for kids hurt by the shrug of the outside world, as though they were not worthy of more. When, as Alex says, you go through life thinking, "Not a lot of people care about other people, you know what I'm saying?"

To be perceived as truly caring, however, the suburban students needed to do more than just feel bad for the Taylor kids. Over the course of the project, Allie came to trust the suburban students were "like caring about it, because they want to know more, and they want to be able to be part of a change." This was also Slim's conclusion, when she said that, from the project, "I learned there's other people that care about the thing you're going through. And there's people that also want to change it, make the same goal." These two pieces were inseparable: caring meant taking action. Alex moved from his bleak belief in an uncaring world after "seeing a whole bunch of people working for the same purpose. It gives you a positive vibe and good feelings."

It's interesting, we spent a lot of time in Metro intentionally supporting relationship-building, thinking this would enhance the students' capacity for shared action. But one of the things we found is that the reverse was also true: engaging in action together strengthened relationships. "We're all doing this project for a reason," Bianca said, "working on something that's common. Wyndham and Taylor students are working on the same thing. So that's already a connection." I hadn't thought of that before, that they would find commonality in the work. "I think because we—like Taylor and Wyndham kids—both want to make a change, that brought us together. And I like the experience I had with them," Angelica said. I found a definition of solidarity in the Oxford Dictionary that references 'unity of feeling or action.' With the suburban kids, the city students felt they had both, and that they were mutually reinforcing.

If this is beginning to feel like those stock photos of diverse kids holding hands, let me deromanticize it a little. There is a disheartening side. The Taylor students gave out extra credit to the suburban kids for being there while not crediting themselves enough.

It started with how educational inequality did not seem to be the suburban students' issue to solve. "It's not their problem," Eddy asserted. "It's not affecting them, it's affecting us," Trina told me. Believing this, the Taylor kids were often stumped when I asked why the Wyndham kids would be involved in the fight for equal schools. "Actually, I don't know why," Mia replied. "Because if you're getting the education, why bother with anybody else's education?" When I asked Lucy, we got caught in a loop. "I don't know, why should they care?," she replied. "I don't know, I'm asking you," I said, laughing. At her turn again, Lucy said, "I don't know why they should care. I mean, they have what they need." Wyndham is more than covered, she's saying. They've got electives, sports arenas, counselors, tutors, teachers with time for office hours, and an iPad in every backpack.

So when the suburban students advocate anyway, without anything apparent to gain, the Taylor students believe they're witnessing a purity of motive. "They have more things and stuff, and they don't *need* to worry about the 'lower' schools—it shows they care," Anthony told me. Lucy decided it was a matter of character. "It's good that they care. I think it's more because the type of person they are that they're doing this." By "them saying things about it" to public figures, Slim believed, "it's like they actually care, even though they're not the ones being affected by what's going on." To the Taylor students, the suburban kids are doing good out of the goodness of their hearts.

I do not mean to minimize the Taylor students' positive feelings for their suburban partners or to diminish the suburban students' commitment. But there is more to be said here. The Wyndham students are direct beneficiaries of opportunities unequally distributed in our society. They have personal experience with inequality, just on its more advantaged end. Fixing it is less a matter of caring or character than a matter of responsibility, to pay down a debt that continues to accrue (Biss, 2015; Ladson-Billings, 2006, p. 5). If our project helped to answer Lucy's question of "Why should they care?" I think that it would add balance to how the city students perceive the partnership they're in. It might help them insist that the suburban students *should* be there, fulfilling their duty to create a just educational system.

It would also change, I think, how the city students see their own role in advocating for equality. Because, disconcertingly, they repeatedly characterized the act of speaking up about their own school as "complaining." They meant this as a self-criticism, worrying they were being selfish, or whining.

The suburban students, the Taylor students believed, could be a buffer from that judgment. "So that the state legislators could see it's not just us complaining about where we live or how our school is," Trina explained.

"They could see we actually need change, and we actually need help. Even the people that's not having any problems believe this is what should happen." It's as though the suburban students legitimate the cause, because, unlike the city students, they have no agenda; educational inequity is not their problem. And so, wanting more for Taylor is not some selfish desire or empty complaint. The need must be real.

But the city students' advocacy for an equal education is legitimate in its own right. Activism in their self-interest is not the same as selfishness (Alinsky, 1971). They have a right to be believed—the need *is* real—and to the opportunities they are pushing for. And anyway, we can tell from their own words how their participation in Metro was never just about themselves. It was also about their younger sisters, brothers, friends, nieces, nephews, cousins, and neighbors. Further, even though the Taylor students are worried about their own school, there are many, many schools in the same position. In Chicago's neighborhood schools, in cities and rural corners around the state, there are thousands of students bumping up against the same limited opportunities. So the Taylor students' activism for school funding equity covers a lot of ground.

The Taylor students seem to have rejected the idea that they are responsible for the insufficient resources at their school. "It's not our fault we're going through this," Trina stated assuredly. Yet they have not yet turned away from the idea that the responsibility for correcting this wrong is theirs alone. If it is not their fault, then the people whose fault it is, and the people who gain short-term, and the people with power to do something—they all have a duty to fix this, too.

Developing Motivation

When I tell people about Metro, the second-most frequent worry I hear, after the concern about the city students feeling bad, is whether their exposure to a suburban school might trigger their educational detachment. That is not the case, and in fact, their school engagement went up. However, I must also report that this is not all benefit. Some of their motivation represents a shouldering of too much of the burden for their success.

When the city students went to the suburban school, they didn't just see gyms and cafeterias and dance classes. They saw suburban students, "always in the library," "doing homework," and even, "studying in the hall."

To them, it appeared the Wyndham kids were "really engaged:" they "put their opinion out there" during class discussions and were "quiet and doing their work" when that was needed. "They really wanted to be there," was the overall impression.

I hate that I'm telling you this because I'm worried that a stereotype may already be starting to form. Or perhaps you're worried about my telling, that I'm beginning to reinforce stereotypical thinking. But I want to be open about what the Taylor students noticed while visiting the suburban school. And in debriefs when they were back in Chicago, and in interviews with me, they repeatedly remarked on the suburban students' apparent studiousness, work ethic, and achievement. "I feel like they are more focused on school," was a frequent comment, and you can see from its construction that the comparison favored Wyndham's student body. This particular remark came from Mia, during a conversation with her Taylor friends. While spending time with the suburban students, she said, "I learned they always try to do their best because they want to get into a good college."

The intensity of this academic investment prompted the Taylor students to try to match it. Maria, for example, believed that the Wyndham students were studying a more advanced curriculum. This was worrying, she said, because "let's be honest, they're our competition when it comes to jobs and college scholarships." It was a race the suburban students seemed poised to win unless she took some individual action. "It makes me want to learn more, and get a better education, so I won't be years behind." For her, this meant, studying harder, and "getting extra work done." Maria's take-home message after seeing Wyndham was, "We got to be on our A game." Uncannily, David used the same sports metaphors as Maria to describe how the project motivated him. "It affected me. Like I want to step my game up. It makes me want to learn more, so I won't feel left out. So I learn as well too." This extra push could help him to catch up to the suburban students, he believed. More student-of-the-month than sportsperson, Jerry reacted to the suburban school with a critique of his own diligence. Seeing the Wyndham students' degree of focus made him decide, "there's a problem, I'm over here just sitting, not doing anything." This is actually not true: he didn't share it, but his friends touted his high ACT score. But still, the suburban school's academic emphasis told him, "I should try harder in my classes, achieve more."

So yes, the project was motivating, but we need to look at the costs. I'm going to note here that all of the Taylor students saw clearly the obvious disparity in resources between the suburban school and theirs. All of them talked about how much Wyndham's supports could help them succeed. The genesis of the disparity—unequal school funding—was familiar by now to all. What I'm trying to say is they'd recently glimpsed the social causes and understood these had effects. But when it came to understanding their own achievement, and that of the suburban kids, it's like they skipped to the next record groove. They relied on an older, more deeply ingrained, individualist understanding, that each person creates their own success.

So convinced were they that in Metro, the Taylor kids saw a gap in achievement, and thought it was their job, and in their capacity, to make it up all on their own. There is something amazing about the spirit of their conviction. All of the students promised they were going to succeed "too;" they would pull alongside. David even aimed to surpass. "I want to show that I could be better than them," he said, although he joked it would take him longer because the old computers at Taylor take forever to turn on. There's a defiance and an 'I'll prove you wrong' aspect to this thinking. There is also, I think, some survivor mentality, a way of reasoning, amid all the other challenges, this unequal resource thing is just one more: 'I will keep my head down, I will succeed.' Jerry showed some of this when he pledged to "take advantage" of his education, "even though, compared to Wyndham, we don't have the same."

But if we step back from the individual kids for a moment, there is blame lurking in the belief that trying harder should be enough to close the gap. They talked about their new efforts and upward achievements so proudly, but I worry their merit ideology got reinforced in Metro, that their interpretation of differences in achievement dragged down their sense of self.

There were two Taylor students who interpreted the academic side of inequality a little more healthily, and they can lead us to a different place. What makes them unique is that they channeled their motivation simultaneously in two directions—towards themselves and towards the school system. Seeing Wyndham, and participating in Metro, Xavia said, "made me more motivated, you could say, and value my education, the little education, the good thing I have. And it sparked a fire in me to speak up and hopefully get the word out that this isn't fair." It's the speaking up about unfairness part that lights a new path. This shows up in Janelle's thoughts as well. "Taking the project and putting it all together," Janelle said, "we're fighting for equality." But, she continued, "We're not going to get it right away. For now, I have to do what I have to do." She resolved that she was "not going to fall behind because it's Taylor." Instead, "the project made me think you have to set a high standard wherever you are, whoever you are, whether you're a Wyndham kid or whether you're a Taylor kid." There is still some relativism, that the expectations should be the same regardless of how much help you have to meet them. Both students are setting themselves up for some heavy lifting. But it sounds healthier because it's fighting back on multiple levels, the social through activism and the individual through personal achievement.

I think this issue comes up whenever we work with students who are marginalized by our current social system. How do we emphasize the necessity of social change, while also asking students to live their best lives in the present? I can't presume to know the answer, but I think Xavia and Janelle point us there: that individual success is a form of self-care, and a position of strength to work from while fighting for change.

Another answer, I hope, is to work on expanding kids' understanding of achievement. What they're witnessing, when they see the academically-competitive, college-obsessed culture at Wyndham, is the accumulation of race, class, and resource advantage. It provides white and wealthier kids with a separate, better-funded education, intensive support inside and outside of school, and all the supplies needed for success. It starts kids farther ahead and then props up that surplus every school year. It gives effort more of a sure payoff, and it protects modest and mediocre efforts. The achievement gap is just as unfair as the gaps in technology, college counseling, and class offerings the Taylor kids saw—because it comes from the same source. The achievement gap is inequality.

And the Taylor kids' own achievement is more than they give credit for. They have many more jobs than being a good student, which is how most of the suburban kids describe their purpose at this stage in life. For starters, the Taylor kids have actual jobs—they are working after school and on weekends literally to support their families. They are taking care of younger sisters and brothers, cooking meals, going grocery shopping, then doing homework. They are worried constantly—about their parents, about the safety of the block they need to walk down, about the money needed for bills or school fees, about the solidity of their futures. They've experienced trauma or have been closely adjacent to it; what comes with discrimination, immigration enforcement, and gun violence.

All of that—and when they come to school, they are also just kids. They are silly and supportive with their friends and sneak style into their school uniforms. They hug each other in the hallways; they go to class and do their work; they participate in discussions and razz their teachers; they play sports; and they audition for the school play. They apply to college, and when they get in, agonize over how to pay for it, and whether they should go far or stay close to their families. Ms. Isabel, the community organizer, calls the Taylor kids survivors, based on all the struggles they contend with, and she likes to highlight their skills in areas where the suburban kids have no experience. The city kids might not notice otherwise, because there is no test that validates the extraordinary effort to be students alongside the rest.

And as for the traditional metrics of achievement—those SATs, GPAs, and more—if we could compensate accurately for all of the obstacles in their way, maybe we could see the results of their efforts. There are some ways to guess at this statistically, but there is no way to do this in real life. In the school system we live in now, socio-economic status, race, and opportunity are inextricably mixed in on students' transcripts. The Taylor kids are survivors against the odds. But the odds are great, and it shouldn't be on students to overcome them. Not without a bigger fight that moves out of the individual arena and takes it to the structures and policies where inequity lives.

And you might think it would be natural for city students to engage that fight, since it is, after all, in their interest to do so. But going to a school that's under such duress can be alienating (Taines, 2012). It's frustrating to bump into constant challenges, and it made them a little mad at their school. They didn't have an understanding before about why this was always happening. "At first, as a student in a high school like this, I'm like, 'I don't want to deal with none of this,'" Lena said. Eddy tried to tune out what was going on around him. "I was like, 'Whatever, I've just got to pass these four years and I'm done.'" Getting through was all that mattered. They weren't going to make the school's problems their problems, if they could help it.

Seeing the school's "faults" as inequity brought about a shift. The "injustice," Angelica said, "made me care about this school and the community." That was the first step, to care about Taylor's welfare. Once those feelings switched on, they wanted to be part of the process. "I started doing this project, and it got me more involved in the school, to help it out," Lali said. Xavia went from a 'forget this place' attitude (actual words: "screw CPS") to wanting to become an activist-educator. "The project really did motivate me a lot more to become a teacher. I'm just really pumped up. I will speak about this," she pledged. While before Eddy had just wanted school to be over with, now he wanted to stay involved. "I still want to be a part of this, I still want to help out," he told me. Metro "gives you a whole different mindset," explained Slim, who'd admitted to negative feelings about Taylor before. It helped her find the good in her school among the hardships. "Stuff like this, it makes you want to hold on to the education part, and fight for it in a way." The Metro experience strengthened the Taylor students' school bond. It made them ready to take up the fight: for themselves, for their school, for their community.

❖

References

Alinsky, S. (1971). *Rules for radicals: A pragmatic primer for realistic radicals.* New York, NY: Random House.

Biss, E. (2015, December 2). White debt: Reckoning with what is owed—and what can never be repaid—for racial privilege. *New York Times Magazine.*

Freire, P. (2006). *Pedagogy of the oppressed* (30th anniversary ed.). New York, NY: Continuum.

Ladson-Billings, G. (2006). From the achievement gap to the education debt: Understanding achievement in U.S. schools. *Educational Researcher, 35*(7): 3–12.

Taines, C. (2012). Intervening in alienation: The outcomes for urban youth of participating in school activism. *American Educational Research Journal,* 49(1): 53–86.

CHAPTER SEVEN

Personal Change: The Wyndham Students

THERE'S BEEN A LOT of public discourse about how to grow empathy, and it's often the Wyndham demographic that's thought of in this talk. How do we get advantaged people—white and wealthier people—to contribute to inequality's un-making? Not with charity or condescension, or some surface diversity talk, but with a genuine desire to understand the harm, and a willingness to put their advantage on the line? An experience like Metro might be part of the answer, because we'll see some of that among the Wyndham kids. We'll also notice how some blind spots remain unseen.

Getting Closer to Inequality

Talk to any young person from a well-off suburb about where they live, and the word 'bubble' will almost invariably come up. The Wyndham students used it constantly: "we are in a kind of bubble." I've thought about that term a lot, about what it means to them. Bubbles are round and floaty, rainbow-covered and clear. I can tell from their choice of words that there is something in them they like: protection, maybe, or a model of a good life, underneath the dome. Even with its downsides, saying you live in a bubble doesn't feel very exclusive. There's nothing hard-sounding about the metaphor, it's no "gated community." Bubbles just aren't that mean. There's a utility in the image in that it can highlight white and wealthy kids' separateness while giving the impression that the world is relatively open and light, invoking birthday parties, green grass, and sunshine. It's a soft-focus description of a problem: bubble walls are thin, but they can circumscribe a life.

Inside the bubble, the Wyndham kids depicted a life of homogeneity. "At least in a ten-mile radius," Olivia noted, "there's nothing really going on, it's just the same kind of people." Their social lives were a closed loop of sameness in economic status, sameness in racial background. "All of the activities I do involve people from this area. I just don't get out in much of the world." Annaliese shared. "When you live in the suburbs, I feel like you're so isolated," Maggie told me.

Of course, this is different from "the box" the Taylor kids described, because the bubble is more of a choice. Wyndham families moved inside it intentionally for the material goods it provides. And they've made the walls around it on purpose, to keep the goods in and the less privileged out. Hence the letters to the editor against proposals to redistribute some state funds for education. Hence the testimony at town meetings against an affordable housing development.

Another way the bubble is different is that it doesn't keep them in one place. The Wyndham students are highly mobile: they have cars, their parents have cars, they fly frequently. I remember sitting with a group of suburban kids after school and listening to them talk about their winter break plans. A student said she was going to Italy and Israel: that's two international trips in two weeks. No one treated this as unusual—her teacher skipped no beats suggesting restaurants and museums to visit.

The suburban students also go to Chicago pretty regularly, to the fancy shopping district near the lake, to Cubs games and Lollapalooza, even to the casually expensive restaurants within ten minutes of Taylor, part of gentrification's first wave. In addition to vacations and outings, the Wyndham students go out-of-state and even abroad for college, a highly admired tradition in their community of "going away for school." But while they've been to the city, and all over the world, the bubble somehow stays with them. "Even if I'm traveling, it's usually I'm with the same sort of people," Annaliese admits. It's like a forcefield that surrounds them wherever they go. "Many people who live here," said Prem, "don't want to get out of this bubble." The bubble is the decision to stay within a particular set of surroundings and in community with a particular set of people. It's the choice to stay at a remove as they move through the world.

This is where the Wyndham students were coming from as they began Metro. "I had no idea about the Chicago Public Schools because of the bubble that surrounds the North Shore," Maya explained. "We don't really understand or know anything about what's going on outside it." Maya's Wyndham peers shared that blinkered sense of reality, saying, "I didn't really see it before;" "I didn't really know;" and "I wasn't really aware of these school funding inequities."

Questioning them further, they did have *some* idea. "I probably knew," Annaliese said, "that not all schools are funded equally," but this remained "somewhere in the back of my mind." The issue stayed there, on the back burner, because it could. It wasn't something that seemed central to their lives under the dome. "Before I was not really as sympathetic," said Jashaundra. "I was like, 'I do care about other people's education, but I have this education.'" It was the same for Maya, her attitude being, "It wasn't something I thought I needed to know. I was like, 'I'm fine. I've never not had these things.'" Educational scarcity was not a part of their reality. And from the comfort of their bubble, the realities hurting Chicago's public schools seemed very far away. Thinking of her vantage point before Metro, Shana said, "I go into the city, or I hear about it on the news, and it seems very distant." The world outside of Wyndham was kind of a blur.

Where did Metro take them? Well first, it took them away from inward-looking suburban sameness. "I've gotten out of my bubble a lot," Jonas said. "I've just come out a more well-rounded person." Metro offered a 360-degree view, an opening out into the world around them. "This program helps Wyndham students be more aware of our surroundings," noticed Ruth. What was happening outside their community became easier to see. Metro "just opened up a whole new window," Claire said. And what they saw from that window was "like a wake-up call, like a sense of reality," stated Maggie.

Hearing this, we can tell that the bubble hasn't gone away exactly, even metaphorically. But with Metro's help, the Wyndham kids went beyond the bubble for a time and took in new vistas. Maybe we can picture their bubble stretching and expanding; it's the kind that goes all wobbly and irregular, no longer a perfectly-contained sphere.

Spending time in a new reality knocked their own school experiences off-center. For Kylie, Metro "opened my eyes to see that maybe not everything is the same" as what she received in the comforts of her own school. It was dawning on the suburban students that their reference points were limited. "I do cross-country so I've been to a lot of different schools, but most are similar to Wyndham," Jashaundra said. In Metro, "that was my first time seeing a city school. I didn't even know how different city schools were," until then. Going to Taylor offered a new vantage point for seeing how far apart their educations were. "I learned a lot," said Jonas, "about the differences in the schools. It helped me put it in perspective. I know the problem exists now." Getting to know a Chicago high school helped them picture the severity of the issue, the scale of the inequality.

Something we need to hold space for and come back to is that "the problem," as the suburban students understood it, was situated in Chicago. For example, Maggie telling me that from Metro, "I learned a lot more about the Chicago school district, how it's funded, how it works." Or Maya who said, "I learned so much: the lack of resources they have, the lack of opportunities they have. So much that needs to be done in the city of Chicago for schools." While the Wyndham kids have taken lessons on inequality, for them that inequality lives in the city—not in their suburban towns.

But what did happen is that, as they visited Taylor over and over, educational inequality shifted from something hazy and off-stage to something up close and personal. "We get to firsthand go see just how big those differences are," Haley explained. And "when you're in that situation yourself, it means so much more to you. It's so much more emotional." It's as if a too-big, far-off problem suddenly crashed into their lives. "I care about the issue more than when I started," shared Elizabeth. The suburban students said they "thought about it more" and "talked about it more" than they ever had before. They became "more interested," "more passionate," more invested in the circumstances of Chicago schools. "I think it changed me," Jashaundra told me, of her time in Metro. "Now I realize it's just so not right. I feel anger towards what's happening and how so many people are deprived of a possible future." Maya also took offense on the Taylor students' behalf. "I definitely got an understanding of where they're coming from," after Metro, she said. "I almost feel what they're feeling. When you see their school, you just feel like, 'How can you not have these things? You need them!'"

When the suburban kids tell me their reactions, it's almost like I can feel them zoom in. They see a school up close; they get to know new kids; and then they're actually there, connecting to the issue. "Chicago and other areas like that aren't so far away," Shana began to feel, "and it's really important that everyone gets a good education."

Recognizing Advantages

Before Metro, the constant motion of suburban existence—classes, after-school clubs, sports, late night homework, and college stress—kept them "captivated by what's going on" in their school bubble. They couldn't see the forest—the larger educational system—but they also didn't pause much to see the trees, the shade and support that their school provided. They passed by it every day, "all the things I have been given without a second thought," as Lisa put it. There was so much at their disposal, it was impossible to keep track of. "Like we have so many things I've never seen before. I don't even have time to use all of this," said Adrianna. Without noticing or experiencing all Wyndham had to offer, without any second thoughts, what tended to happen is they simply got used to the abundance—it was everyday unremarkable. "I kind of took everything for granted," Adrianna admitted. There were some shiny things that stood out—the glass arts studio and the radio station. But they especially didn't notice the people who were all around them—the counselors, teachers, therapists, tech support staff, and more, creating a literal social safety net. Prior to Metro, Abbey said, "I took them for granted because I only thought of inequality as how much school supplies you have." So the Wyndham kids went on about their day without having a true measure of how much they actually had going for them.

Part of the journey of Metro was "getting a grasp of what they do not have" at Taylor "that we have." And after traveling to a school with less, the suburban students came back to Wyndham better able to see their more. The offerings at their school moved from the background to the foreground. "Now I don't take everything for granted," Adrianna told me, following Metro. The lesson went beyond simple acknowledgement of the resources lifting them up. Instead, Metro precipitated a cherishing of the suburban school's opportunities. "It made me appreciate everything at Wyndham more," said Abbey. "I just learned to be grateful for what I have," said Sarah. This sentiment, this gratitude for their suburban education, was a constant reference after Metro. "I feel like I've grown as a person from understanding how much privileges and advantages I receive and how blessed I am," reflected Caitlin.

Part of what counted as 'appreciative' to the suburban students was not leaving so much of what they had on the table, unused. Doing Metro "has made me feel I need to take advantage of my education as much as I can," Haley told me. This meant seeking out more of the enrichments available in the far corners of the school. When we went on the school tour, many of our Wyndham guides admitted this was their first time seeing things like the rock climbing wall, the robotics lab, or the ceramics kiln—even though they were in the building every day. Her senior year, after focusing almost entirely on traditional college prep, Adrianna finally decided to take an art class, a direct result of learning "it's an experience I don't think I would've had at Taylor." It was a resolve to "try to use all of the resources that are given to me," Shana explained, after becoming "a lot more grateful for everything I'm given."

The adults in their lives were perpetually harping on this same message. "I've always heard from teachers and parents how great Wyndham was, how many opportunities that we have that other schools don't," remarked Jonas. Perhaps families and schools wanted more thanks for their efforts to provide, since wealth was all the Wyndham kids knew and they may not notice otherwise. Or perhaps this was an effort to develop character, to cultivate humbleness rather than blasé expectation. But whatever the motivation, and despite being constant recipients of this admonition, it was Metro that drove home the gratitude.

And yet, while being thankful for what one has is needed, it is not exactly a radical act. It suggests a complacency, an 'I'll hang onto this but just appreciate it more,' or worryingly, 'take advantage of it more.' It is a cul de sac in the bubble rather than a road out towards equity.

For something we can tell from the Wyndham kids' newfound gratefulness is that they're not very troubled by what they have. Unlike when they're in the city, they do not take in the scene at their school and think, 'this is so unfair.' They do not recognize the resources gushing in every direction as being unequal. Instead, at the end of their tenure in Metro, I heard statements such as these from the suburban students: "We're not directly influenced by this inequality;" "we're not personally affected by it, but we still care;" "we're outside, like a third party that is not affected by the problem—that would be Wyndham in this situation."

In the most literal sense, I can see what they mean. They are not going without college counselors or books, they are not subjected to hallway surveillance. It would be disingenuous for the suburban kids to say they know what it's like, on a daily direct basis, to attend a low-funded city school.

But unaffected? Their school is a mirror image of the one they visited in Chicago; they are in the same system. The reason why Taylor has too little is the same reason why Wyndham has so much. They are not outsiders to inequity, they are just on "the haves" side, receiving all that support, plus more.

The suburban students, didn't see it this way, though, even after Metro. And that's because they subscribe to an almost mystical story about the origins of their suburban upbringing. In this telling, the genesis of their advantage is: luck.

In the beginning, a person-to-be is given a random ticket in what Adrianna called the "geographical lottery." The wheel of life spins around, and then, "it's luck of the draw, where you were born," Jonas said. By happenstance, a child could end up in the suburbs, with wealthy parents and well-funded schools. "I'm just lucky to be where I am. I'm lucky to be a student at Wyndham," said Maggie gratefully. Or, if the ticket is not quite as golden, a child could end up in lower-income places with schools that have less than they need. "If I was born to a mom and dad that live in the Taylor community, how different my life would be," realized Adrianna. The chance to be educated at Wyndham—"anyone could have it and anyone couldn't," Sarah "realized," and she was "grateful" for lucking out.

The story might be true in the cosmic sense: the chance that a soul becomes embodied as a child in a suburban family *is* probably random. (I don't know how to compute those odds.) But nothing else about this is. If we returned to the more sociological-historical origin story, we'd have to point to discrimination in bank lending, freeway development, zoning ordinances, real estate selling, town planning, district boundary-making—only a partial list!—to explain how these kids ended up on a segregated island at a well-funded school (McGhee, 2021; Owens & Rich, 2023; Rothstein, 2017). We'd dig down even farther to what the Metro community organizers call "root causes:" racism and classism. We'd need to add not just our historical knowledge but our attention to the present-day: the suburban news editorials against funding equity, the backlash against affordable housing, the lobbying of elected officials to vote for "suburban" interests.

However, when the prevailing narrative is "luck," it's no wonder the suburban students see themselves as "unaffected" by inequality. Inequality in this thinking is misfortune, something they'd magically escaped. It was the city students who, unluckily, came into the world with educational hardship at their door.

The change in the Wyndham students during Metro occurred within this tight story arc. But it was a change. Where they landed was a desire to share what they saw as their good fortune. To spread it around to the benefit of the Taylor students. "Hopefully," Lisa said, "we can make other kids just as lucky to get the same education as us." Instead of walling off their resource-riches, the suburban students wanted to ensure that city students received them, too. "We're not like, 'We just want to keep it for ourselves,'" said Elizabeth of her education at Wyndham. "No, we want everyone to feel the experience."

To help make that happen, the Wyndham students made a kind of deal with themselves: they were willing to give up some of their advantages for the public good. The bargain seemed to start with a sense that there is a core set of must-haves for any school, but Wyndham had a layer of "extras" above that line. "They give us more than we need," was Sarah's perspective. "It's actually too much." The add-ons created room for compromise, a surplus that could be applied towards equity. Prem proposed "directing more resources from suburbs, like say Wyndham or Grandview, into their schools. 'Cause honestly, we don't need as much as we have here." In their meetings with state legislators, Sarah, Shana, Jashaundra, and Annaliese suggested the reallocation of Wyndham's state funds to lower-income schools. The local property taxes in Wyndham, they said, already funded their school more than enough.

In the popular parlance of progressive circles, the cause of justice requires white and wealthy students 'to give up their privilege.' The Wyndham students, we can see, did not go that far. They didn't want to part with anything that cut too close to the bone of what they considered necessary for their learning or their futures. They wanted to keep most of what they had. It might seem impossible, then, for the Wyndham students to have both—their education as-is and a better-resourced education for the Taylor kids. But they disagreed with the zero-sum construction of the problem that says for others to have more, they would have to have less. "I think no one's education should be lessened," Shana told a state legislator. "Everyone's education should be brought up. Everyone deserves the same opportunities as

Wyndham." They didn't see their school as a privilege, true, but they also did not believe it was their exclusive prerogative. Instead, they felt strongly that the educational opportunities coming their way should be extended to all. And the only way to square that circle was through activism—to demand, alongside the Taylor students, that the state come up with the funds and resources to bring city schools up to equity.

Taking a break at Wyndham High. Photo courtesy of author.

Developing Activists

It's often said you can't make someone care, but here we see a process—over a year, or two—of suburban students caring more deeply about the obstacles city students encounter at school. We'd be concerned, however, if the Wyndham students simply stayed in their feelings. That doesn't do anything to alter the facts on the ground. In Metro, the suburban kids' emotions carried them towards action. "Before, I might think, this is really sad," Annaliese said, and the response would end there. "Now when I hear something about this," the educational barriers kids at Taylor face, "I'm like, 'That's bad, what can I do or what can we do to fix that?'" Learning about educational disparity in close-up was not a passive or cerebral exercise for the suburban kids. Instead, as Noa said, "it opened my eyes to the inequalities in school funding and made me want to do something. It definitely inspired me to take action." They could cite per pupil funding and discuss property taxes. But that wasn't the core content of Metro. "Really the main thing I learned from it," said Prem, "is motivation to change something."

Metro is an action project, and the Wyndham kids took their inspiration into letter-writing and testifying. But the Wyndham kids also engaged in advocacy on their own, inside their suburban spaces. They incorporated the lessons of Metro into class presentations and talked frequently with friends and family. It was like they were trying to recreate the experience for those who didn't go on the trips: by sharing the details of disparity and inciting a drive to do something.

But first they had to convince them. Because this was an activism occurring in the belly of the beast, with communities intentionally invested in the system we have now.

"I learned about their school, about urban cities in general, and how funding in Illinois worked," Brian said of his time in Metro. "Because I'm sure my parents know," he continued, "but I had no idea." I want us to picture it: Wyndham students learning about school funding for the first time, going to see Taylor, and viewing the mammoth gap up close. They go home to express their shock and . . . it turns out their parents already know.

In fact, their parents have made key life decisions based on this knowledge: where to build a home, where to send their kids to school. "My parents moved to Wyndham 15 or 16 years ago because of the educational opportunities," Jashaundra said. And when she tried to talk to them about the issue: "They're not complete supporters of it. They want educational equality, but also . . ." She stopped, interrupting herself. "Actually, I don't know if they want it," she said. "I think they think," like many in Wyndham, "'I'm paying this much to live here, I'm paying this much for my kid to go to school.'" But Jashaundra made clear: "I don't agree with that."

This is a tough spot that left Jashaundra feeling torn. But the important thing is: she is having this conversation, and her parents are hearing an alternate position.

And what's interesting here is that, at Jashaundra's urging, her family hosted a brunch for her Taylor partners, during a year when we did home visits. Just before the city students arrived, Jashaundra's mom "was being really weird about it," asking, "'Isn't it dangerous to have people over?'" Jashaundra replied, "Mom, you're going to meet them and you're going to be like, 'Why did I ever think that?'" And she was right. "They came over and they're just like normal teenagers. And she's like, 'Oh. Those girls are just like you.'"

We would hope the humanity of city students would be assumed, but clearly in these isolated and segregated communities, stereotypes run deep. So this may be a low bar, but Jashaundra's continued, self-described "arguments" with her parents, and her parents' interactions with the Taylor students, resulted in a small shift in perspective. I know it's a hopeful leap, but these attitude adjustments could create more openness to the kinds of policy changes required to get to equity.

Perhaps I'm hopeful because several Wyndham students reported similar dynamics—how they worked on family members during the project, and saw some movement.

For example, Sarah shared the back-and-forth with her family. "Even talking to my parents, they want to help, but at the same time, my dad also brought up some good points." Any changes to school funding, her father believed, would result in a need to raise taxes in the suburbs to recoup Wyndham's losses. "Adding that amount of money on him," her dad said, "would affect our lives." ("We're not the wealthiest, but we're not struggling to live in Wyndham" either, Sarah clarified to me.) Sarah told her dad she supported the redistribution of state funds and dramatic policy change. The pushback, though, was illuminating. "I was able to see my view on it, but think about how it will affect my community, too."

So Sarah's idealism was a little caught in the middle, between Metro's inspiration and her community's opposition. But we can see the remnants of a real exchange—how she's talking about the inequities she saw, and advocating to her parents for a real solution.

And she went one step further: she invited them to attend an end-of-the-year event for Metro, where Taylor and Wyndham students presented a student bill of rights. There, her parents heard from the city students directly, which created more of an impression than "hearing me tell them." The denial of opportunity was no longer a fact from afar. And "after we left," Sarah said, "My parents, they're like, 'We're going to make sure this is known, like the struggles. People need to know.'" This marks, perhaps, the steps of one Wyndham family away from the sidelines of continued inequality.

Meanwhile, Annaliese was working on the next generation. She'd heard from the Taylor teachers and students about the damage the Chicago mayor caused by closing 50 schools in Black and Latino neighborhoods. Back home, she picked up the story. "I'll be in the car with my brother, driving somewhere," she said. "This actually happened. The news about the school closings came on, and we started this huge debate about it. He's a freshman, so he doesn't really care. I was like, 'No, Stephen, you have to understand. Let me tell you about educational inequity in school funding.'" I don't know the end of this story, we'll have to see how Stephen grows up. But I know it's better that he heard it.

Developing Solidarity

The Wyndham students in Metro didn't need convincing. They'd visited Taylor and gotten to know the Taylor kids. They'd felt the pain, vicariously, of blocked opportunity. Rather than remaining outside the circle, they were moved to ask, as Maya did, "How do we solve this now?!" The Metro experience helped the Wyndham students find that "we:" the collective will to fix educational inequality, with them very much included. "We're here because we're not ok with this either," Jonas stated. "We care about this too," said Caitlin. Letting the Taylor students fend for themselves wasn't an option. "We don't want to go our separate ways and have each of us go through our own struggles," said Prem. Instead, they were taking a "united sort of stand," Annaliese said, a public affirmation of how "we need a change, and everybody thinks so. It's not just one school."

So they set out together to fight this fight. Something their presence added, the Wyndham students believed, was the embodiment of a well-resourced education. When the Taylor students testified to what was missing, what they needed, and what they wished for, the Wyndham students were there to show that such a school exists. They enacted the other pole and made visible the gap in-between. "It's kind of a point of comparison," Laila explained. "Wyndham is here to say, when we go talk to legislators, 'this is what Taylor should have also.'" These are the resources that the Taylor students should have, too.

The Wyndham students additionally saw themselves as backup, echoing the Taylor students' truths. "We can corroborate every single thing the Taylor students say," said Jonas, almost as if they were witnesses at a trial. "After Taylor says what they saw, we can say the differences we saw, and doubly fuel the fire for educational equality." Combined they could prove the system's wrongdoing as a way of sparking change.

An intention of Metro, in bringing these two communities together, was to explore how the power of wealth and whiteness could be used in new ways. If this power can so universally and successfully engineer injustice, then perhaps, if harnessed for good, it can be a force for justice. There were a few Wyndham students in Metro who recognized this potential, who saw how their activism beckoned the attention of lawmakers to the cause of equal schools. Jashaundra, for example, observed how "rich people" and white people are more likely to be featured "on the front page" because their lives are deemed more significant. By the same logic, suburban students are more likely be noticed by people in power. "For us, when we advocate for this," Jashaundra said, "it shows the people they think are important care about this." Legislators will tune in to the message of white and wealthy families, Jashaundra is saying, because these are the constituencies they most value. Adrianna agreed that "money goes into all of this," and makes it more likely that the "senators don't push you aside, so they realize the importance of this."

I know this feels awful, this judgment of who is most worthy by our elected officials, this knowingness by suburban youth who are the recipients of that judgment. But they are acknowledging something real about our politics and playing on legislators' biases. It's a bait-and-switch of focus towards equity.

Most of the Wyndham students, though, believed they turned heads not because of who their parents were, but because of their surprising selflessness. *They* didn't need more resources, after all. The generosity of fighting for students who did—that was enough to shock a state rep's conscience. "If Wyndham is like, 'Hey we care about this,' they'll be like, 'Outsiders?! What?! Why do you care?!,'" prodding them to realize, "'Maybe I should too.'" At least in Caitlin's imagining of a lawmaker's internal dialogue.

This thinking can be traced back to the Wyndham students' origin story: their belief that the suburbs exist in a world apart from inequity. And since most people focus on their own needs, the suburban students feel they stand out in their defense of others'. "If it's coming from Wyndham students who have it, and we're arguing for other people's funding, I think that's a powerful message" to the powers that be, said Jonas.

The unfortunate flipside of characterizing themselves as selfless is that it positions the Taylor students, inaccurately, as selfish, or at least hints they may be perceived in this way. "If it was just coming from Taylor, obviously they want more money," Haley said. So regular is it for people to want more for themselves, their requests can easily be dismissed. Or, alone, the city students may appear needy. "If you hear just Taylor's view," said Sarah, "it's going to sound like begging." I also heard the concern that they could be interpreted as "complaining" or "whining it's not fair." All negative dispositions with built-in justifications for not listening. The Wyndham students' magnanimity, they argued, could force a hearing of the unfairness. Since none of these traits applied to them.

There's a germ of truth here in that the Taylor students, and students from similar schools in city and rural places, *are* routinely unheard and overlooked by elected officials. But the suburban students are mistaken about why. It's not that electeds have heard it all before or think those disadvantaged by the system are just griping (although they may use these as excuses). It's that the Taylor community is mostly Latino and low-income, with less social power, and is actively marginalized—treated as less and given less by state and local government.

By the same token, the suburban students, or most of them anyway, mistake why they're heard by misconstruing their power. Wealthy and white suburbs possess the social currency to drive much of the legislative agenda and their representatives' campaigns. What was surprising to the legislators we interacted with in Metro was not the suburban community's selfless generosity but the use of its power for educational equity. Rather than the things it's usually used for: favorable treatment, gatekeeping, and wealth upon wealth.

It's like the Wyndham students are unclear about how their backgrounds affect how they're seen by local officials—or perhaps they're uncomfortable admitting to it.

But a few of them had an inkling of the influence of this community, and believe they'll grow into its power. They expect to be adults on similar terms as their parents—wealthy, holding a résumé of credentials, and carrying clout. With a twist: at least for now, they believe their future selves will use that leverage to create equal schools. "Soon," said Prem, a senior at Wyndham, "I am going to have enough resources at my hand to do more. When that happens, I want to make a change." It's breathtaking really, this assumption of status, but they have the comfort of thinking it cannot go otherwise. And they are mentally putting at least some of their imagined future assets towards the cause.

For Wyndham students are also conscious of their school's legacy, how many of its alumni have gone on to prominent positions in government, business, athletics, and the arts. So it's not just money but also a position of power that they anticipate using to equity's gain. "In the future, if we become big shots and politicians, which I'm sure a lot of my classmates will end up being, we'll make the difference," Ruth declared, a little tongue-in-cheek, but also, serious.

Whether their influence derives from status or selflessness, the Wyndham students believe they are sharing it with the Taylor students, to help fix Chicago's under-funded schools. As they see it, they're joining someone else's fight.

Saul Alinsky (1971), the veteran organizer, said people first need to find their self-interest, or what we might more modernly call "their stake," in an issue before they can commit to changing it. At the end of Metro, it seems many Wyndham students are confused about their community's self-interest in the system as it is. They don't fully see how much educational inequality "helps" them, how much they benefit. And, with everything they get, they'd have to look hard to see how they are also harmed—not as much as the Taylor students, mind you, but harmed nonetheless. And this is important, because without knowing their stake in the current system, it will be harder to find their stake, and their responsibility, in changing it.

All of this may sound like a big burden for teenaged kids, something that may end in defensiveness and guilt rather than action. To prevent that, Mr. Ryan from Taylor likes to tell the Metro students: "You didn't create these systems; you just exist in them." But one time Ms. Sofia, the community organizer, retorted, "Yeah, but someone did."

The intention is not to blame the Wyndham kids but to help them understand they are inside an unequal system that was built intentionally to create their advantages. And, it is constantly being rebuilt by communities like theirs to keep hold of that advantage.

This is the suburban stake in educational *inequality*: the boost it brings to suburban kids who go to schools like Wyndham. For all that they receive, it also harms them, as only one Wyndham Metro student pointed out. What happens in a city school like Taylor, "I guess it also impacts us," Jade told me, "if we're in our own bubble and isolated."

Without this analysis—of how the system helps and harms them, of how it was created and how it's maintained—the Wyndham students frame their activism for educational equality as altruism. Like this, from Annaliese at the end of a project year: "It's not necessarily our problem, but it's something we should be interested in fixing anyway, because it gives all students a better chance at success." Or this from Caitlin, after two years in Metro: "Not being rude, but improving the education of someone at Taylor does not help me. But I'm doing it because I want other people to succeed, being a human being, caring about the world." Altruism sounds sweet but it's flimsy; it's almost certainly not enough to sustain a systems-defying activism. As Alinsky (1971) reminds us, people need to feel the issue matters *to them*, so that they have a personal stake in seeing it change.

Since it looks like they may need help seeing why educational equity is their fight too, here are some reasons: The suburban students have the chance to undo a wrong that they are intimately connected to—it is their problem; it is their "debt" (Biss, 2015, Ladson-Billings, 2006, p. 5). Rather than blindly accepting their school's unjust benefits, they can begin to meet their responsibility for changing the system, in better alignment with a moral life (Biss, 2015, Ladson-Billings, 2006). They can counteract their bubble of isolation, and find community, by being in solidarity with the city students (McGhee, 2021). They can turn wealth and whiteness into a positive force for social change. They can feel good about seeing things shift, a little, slowly, within the school system, within their families, based on what they do.

All of this can assist the Wyndham kids in locating their stake in creating educational equity. Otherwise, if they are only "doing it for others," they will miss what it does for them, and for the metropolitan community they're a part of.

❖

References

Alinsky, S. (1971). *Rules for radicals: A pragmatic primer for realistic radicals.* New York, NY: Random House.

Biss, E. (2015, December 2). White debt: Reckoning with what is owed—and what can never be repaid—for racial privilege. *New York Times Magazine.*

Ladson-Billings, G. (2006). From the achievement gap to the education debt: Understanding achievement in U.S. schools. *Educational Researcher, 35*(7): 3–12.

McGhee, H. (2021). *The sum of us: What racism costs everyone and how we can prosper together.* New York, NY: One World.

Owens, A. & Rich, P. (2023). Little boxes all the same? Racial-ethnic segregation and educational inequality across the urban-suburban divide. *RSF Journal of Social Sciences.* 9(2): 26–54.

Rothstein, R. (2017). *The color of law: A forgotten history of how our government segregated America.* New York, NY: Liveright.

PART IV CODA

The Metro Students' Journey

How can we help kids really see the educational inequality around them? The Taylor students did it by going to the suburbs, by zooming out until the whole system came into view. The Wyndham students got there by forming a connection with a Chicago school, by zooming in so the issue wouldn't feel so far away.

Metro provided the transportation. Not just the bus itself (although we did do that), but a vehicle in the metaphorical sense, if you'll indulge me, for experiencing these disparate schools, connecting the students who attended them, and talking about the differences.

Really being there was crucial for both groups of kids. The city students got a shock from visiting Wyndham, but they said they needed to go, to "notice things going on out there in the world." A culturally competent curriculum is always important, but for the suburban students, "being in the situation" brought them closer to Taylor's reality.

What they got from their travel into other students' lives depended on where they began. The city students journeyed into something like critical consciousness (Freire, 2006). Freire's aim, in a more liberated pedagogy, is for people to separate enough from their oppressive reality in order to see it for what it is. When we listen to the Taylor kids talk about the experience of being away, of spending time in the suburban school, that seems about right. Even the metaphor of sight works. "It opened my eyes to an injustice. Like, I didn't know there was an injustice, but I realized." "Knowing what I can be offered at Wyndham, it's like I see the unfairness." As these sightings crystallize, they are calling out the system, "naming" it, as Freire would say, as unfair and unjust (Freire, 2006, p. 88).

The suburban students arrived at something like empathy. Their reaction to the resources denied at the city school was "personal" and "emotional," as if they could "almost feel" what it was like. That emotional connection extended their care, to include kids and schools beyond the "bubble" of their everyday well-advantaged lives. They got a feel for the city students' school day, which helped them identify with facing school obstacles, even though that wasn't their experience.

Both the city and the suburban students came back to school with new perspective. The Taylor students had been "so used to this, we think it's normal." Their school situation was, borrowing from Freire again, "a given," they'd accepted it—uncomfortably—as "how it was." (Freire, 2006, p. 99). With their new eyes, their critical consciousness, the city students saw the "limits" imposed on their school and decided, "this is not ok." They had a ready image of the kind of school they wanted, and felt strongly about their right to it, declaring, "We do deserve an equal opportunity."

When the suburban students got home to Wyndham, they couldn't continue to take all their resources as a given—not after seeing what the city students had (and didn't have). Metro forced them to stop and notice, to "not take everything for granted," and instead uncomfortably admit "the advantages" they receive. Wanting to share their newly acknowledged good fortune, they expressed openness to redirecting the excess towards students, like their city partners, with greater need.

Going back and forth between these two schools created a desire to do something. For the city students, the shock of abundance, the realization of what was possible in the realm of education, made them want to "fight for it." For the suburban students, the unfamiliar squeeze of constraint made them want to push against it.

The transition from motivation to action is often tricky for youth (and adults). It's hard to know what to do, or how. Metro provided transportation on this too, a way of getting from here to there, by creating campaigns the Taylor and Wyndham kids could engage in together. The city kids said these actions made them feel stronger, to be able "to stand up" and know "we have power." The suburban kids already felt like they had power, given their families' position. The Metro actions taught them about its use as a force for equity, to draw legislators' attention to the needs of city schools.

In the meantime, the Metro kids sped off ahead of where the project was taking them. Kids in each school talked to parents, siblings, friends, and relatives about educational disparity and its wrongness. They were "spreading awareness" everywhere, creating little ripples and, in the process, practicing their advocacy, growing their commitment.

Which is good because they had an eye on the future too. The city kids' push for equity was always for the next generation: the people close to them who they knew deserved more. They said they'd stay with it as adults, and for some, as teachers, so that "other kids can have the opportunities to do what I wanted to do." The suburban kids promised their change efforts would continue in adulthood too, backed up by the clout they expected to accumulate. They'd push for policy changes many in their community opposed—like redistributing public funds and asking wealthy places to increase their share.

In this, the suburban students were pledging to be allies with the city students, to take a "united sort of stand" that shows "we care about this too." The city students could feel this care; it was significant to them that the suburban students were on their side. "We—like Taylor and Wyndham kids—both want to make a change, that brought us together." Metro cultivated solidarity between kids from separate communities, drawing them closer while they acted for equality.

But beliefs about who was affected by school disparities show the limits of that solidarity. Both groups felt the suburban students lived outside the zone of inequity, and therefore had no moral obligation to fix it. The harm, and the fixing, was assumed to be the city students' territory. As a result, students from both places unduly complimented the suburban students' activism and mistakenly made the city students out to be less-admirably self-interested.

What this did was miss the suburban community's role in forming a system in their favor, and thus, their responsibility for undoing a harmful advantage. It also under-credited the generosity of the city students' fight for justice, overlooking their action for younger kids and kids they'll never know. And it missed the city students' bravery, the stepping forward into an arena that marginalizes and disbelieves them.

These misrecognitions show the edges of Metro's outcomes, the places where our support and guidance need to extend beyond.

❖

Reference

Freire, P. (2006). *Pedagogy of the oppressed* (30th anniversary ed.). New York, NY: Continuum.

PART V

The Metropolitan Community

Transformation of the world implies . . . two actions: denouncing the process of dehumanization and announcing the dream of a new society.

—Paulo Freire

CHAPTER EIGHT

Conclusion with Next Steps

The Promise of a Metropolitan School Partnership

THE EVIDENCE IS IN: increasing school funding will lift students' chances in school, college, and life (Candeleria and Shores, 2019; Hyman, 2017; Jackson et al., 2016; Jackson, 2020; LaFortune et al., 2018; Roy, 2011). Higher funding will lift up low-income students, multilingual learners, and students with disabilities even more (Baker, 2018; Baker et al. 2022; Jackson, 2020; Knight et al., 2022; Owens, 2023). With such a strong research base, "you'd think," as Allie from Taylor initially believed, that "everyone would be working on this." Yet knowing how much school funding matters is not enough to free our public educational system from the status quo. The politics of advantage and a numbing normalcy are locking unequal school funding in place. *The Metropolitan Community* presents a new possibility for breaking us out of this cycle: a city-suburban school partnership for educational equity.

Advantage & Apathy

In conversations about educational inequality, attention is rightfully shined on those most harmed by it. But the other half of the equation is sometimes left in the dark: the schools and students benefiting. Attending to this side of the divide is important because it helps us locate the powers that help to keep the cycle going. In our outer-ring suburbs, the geographies most likely to enjoy abundant school funds (Lichter et al., 2023; Owens & Rich, 2023), the families who live there are not always supportive of change. Like one of the Wyndham students said of her parents, "I don't know if they want it. I think they think, 'I'm paying this much to live here; I'm paying this much for my kid to go to school.'" Far-suburban families with means are invested in the current system, as it is serving the kids who get to go to school there (Darling-Hammond, 2013; Massey, 2008; Siegal-Hawley, 2016).

The alarm of affluent suburban parents over talk of equalizing school funding does not go unnoticed by politicians. The view "up in the north suburbs" is that "it's a risk to share the wealth in the educational system," Representative Miske told the Metro students. How would he know? Because "in my line of work, the loudest and squeakiest wheels get heard," and the clout of this constituency raises their volume. In fact, Senator Bauer admitted, very little else breaks through the noise. "We legislators are surrounded by the people who have resources; these people have more access." And when they "come to us and say, 'It worked out for me, the system is awesome, don't worry, it doesn't need to change,'" with enough repetition (and donations), "that shapes our worldview." For legislators who might be persuaded to support funding equity proposals, the pushback can be enough to return them to their original positions. And that's for state representatives sympathetic to the cause. There are of course many others whose political priorities never aligned with city students' experiences, who might "say they care about education in those mailers," Senator Cowan observed, "but then they get to the legislature and it's clear that they don't." The susceptibility of state politicians to the influence of wealth, and political agendas that don't include equity, is how an educational system that hurts so many stays in place for the few (Baker et al., 2020; Darling-Hammond, 2013; Ryan, 2010).

Decades of accrued inequality, of funding disparities being all we know, have settled into hopelessness that the school system can ever change. When every educational institution they'd known was "low-funded and everything," city students like Eddy absorbed the idea "that that's regular when it comes to schools." It felt hard, and not right, but "we think that's the norm." A highly-funded education, meanwhile, seemed automatic to the suburban students, so much so that resources like a climbing wall felt like a shrug: "like, oh, school." Without direct experience with restricted funds, the problem seemed "very distant," allowing an apathetic remove. "I was like, 'I'm fine; I've never not had these things,'" Maya from Wyndham said. Legislators too subscribed to apathy and defeatism. While Representative Reyes conceded that relying on property wealth to fund schools was "wrong," she went on to characterize change as impossible. "It's disheartening, but we couldn't pass something. I'm sorry I don't have an answer for you." It is difficult to muster energy for change when you think nothing will, when disparity seems stuck in place (Freire, 1998; Orfield, 2013).

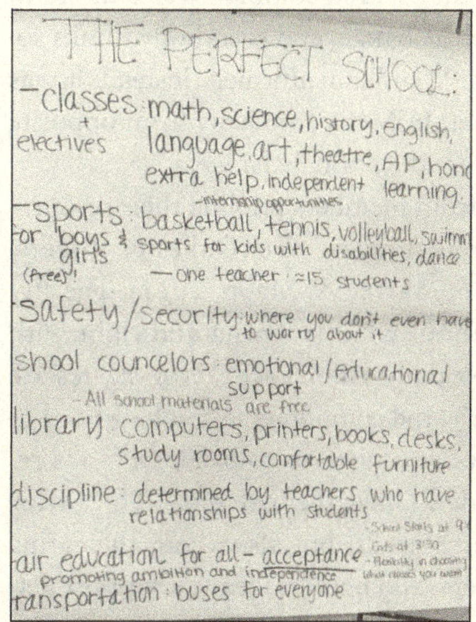

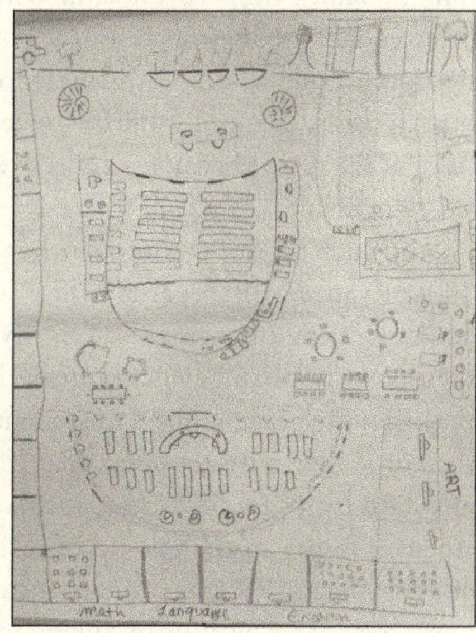

The Metro students' dream school.

New Politics, New Hope

The Metropolitan Community is the first book about a city-suburban school partnership, a new kind of politics for educational equity. The partnership nurtures solidarity, borrows strength from each school community, and amplifies the power of the students' advocacy.

Changing school funding requires changing state law, which means convincing legislators who represent a wide range of communities, from croplands to subdivisions to apartment towers. Persuading such a broad spectrum of elected officials—and counteracting the narrow and outsized influence of wealthy residents—requires a broad-base of constituents to rally (Ryan, 2010). These constituents, however, are separated by geography and life experience, race and economic status, without a venue to come together on needed social change. The city-suburban school partnership is a place to find that alignment and build a wider base. By creating shared space to talk and learn, and experience another kid's school life, the partnership fosters a mutual sense of purpose. "We're all doing this project for a reason, working on something that's common. Wyndham and Taylor are working on the same thing," Bianca from Taylor said. What they had in common was a desire to bring equality to their schools. "We need a change, and everybody thinks so. It's not just one school," Annaliese from Wyndham affirmed. Instead, it was both schools, city and suburban together. In Metro, students from opposite sides of the divide became a collective for educational change.

The richness of a collective comes from members pooling their resources, and each school community has something to give (Oakes & Rogers, 2006; Ryan, 2010; Siegal-Hawley, 2016; Warren & Mapp, 2011). The city students bring intense moral clarity about what is wrong and right with their education, and evidence from their daily attendance. "Our classes are packed with large numbers of students;" "the computers take a half-hour to turn on;" "we only get one nurse;" "we're limited in counselors;" "it's really hard for us to do labs because we don't have the material." The Taylor students testify to the pile-up of resource needs, but also about the caring ethos of their school, as students, teachers, and parents weave a support network together. The ethic of "living for others" is present in the surrounding neighborhood as well, in the heritage of local organizing and community advocates' expertise in people power. The city students bring a fierce urgency to the activism they learn there, cutting through policymakers' attempts to excuse and stall. "Something *has* to be done," Janelle told Representative Miske. "So how can we get all of the legislators to agree? What are your ideas for us?" The question demands an answer from politicians who've long evaded responsibility.

From the suburbs, the kids can testify to what it's like to attend a school that provides almost everything they need: the "crazy options" for history that enliven the subject, the librarians who are "super-helpful" during research assignments, the full-time nurses, the counselors who can provide "individual attention" on college applications. It's a testament to what is possible when schools are funded to maximally support a young person's education. The suburban students also pull the weight of their families' social status into the coalition. "Money goes into all of this," Adrianna admitted, about the Wyndham students' presence at the table. "So the senators don't push you aside." The wealth and privilege in the Wyndham students' backgrounds makes it harder for lawmakers to ignore the collective's call to action. Affluent communities are also more amenable when the message comes from within. "Let me tell you about educational inequity in school funding," Annaliese insisted to a family member. "You have to understand." The suburban students are often related to the opposition and can work on them from the inside.

These are the tools our Metro students carry into a city-suburban partnership.

Partnering across the divide magnifies the city and suburban students' power (McGhee, 2021; Siegal-Hawley, 2016). "After Taylor says what they saw, we can say the differences we saw, and doubly fuel the fire for educational equality," Jonas said of the Metro effect. It is this 'doubling' that strengthens their activism: when two school communities "corroborate" the disparity and jointly call for equity. It's not only the greater numbers that matter; it's the voices of students from such separate places that build resonance, reaching higher heights than either could do apart.

The city-suburban partners modeled their new politics for an institution that, by legislators' own admission, is "too divided" and "removed." The Metro alliance brought a cross-section of legislators to the table: conservative and liberal, rural, urban, and suburban. In district conference rooms and at the state capitol, lawmakers heard emotional testimony about unequal schooling and felt the collective's pressure to act. The message spread further to committee hearings, the senate floor, radio and TV. It looked like "a start of a movement within the legislature," with representatives forming "their own coalitions" across the divides of geography and party. There were, of course, other powers acting on state leaders too: rightward and wealthy residents pushing for a stop; community activists and educators adding to the momentum. Eventually, the Metro-involved legislators together voted 'yes,' along with two 'presents,' on a bill that advanced school funding equity. Among the elected officials the Metro students spoke with, there wasn't a single 'nay.' The coalition held even for suburban, small town, and Republican-leaning members, and those who'd earlier expressed skepticism and defeat.

The bill passed. The new law increased the funds going towards public education and changed the formula so that schools enrolling more low-income, multilingual, and special education students received more to meet their needs. The vote was close—it almost went down to defeat—and so every little bit helped. Including the Metro students' bit. The policy changes they helped bring into being show the promise of a metropolitan partnership.

That promise was felt by the students, too. With each change action they undertook, the city and suburban students confirmed for themselves that an unequal education was not simply the backdrop to their lives. It was not something to tune out and tolerate while they went to class, ate lunch, and did their homework. Belonging to a school partnership, and confronting real policymakers, "made me feel like I could actually do something," Angelica from Taylor said, "because I stood up for what I believe." The stands the Metro students took together dislodged earlier feelings of resignation. Instead of being stuck with an unjust system, they were part of a movement (Freire, 1998). "We are together, two schools, fighting for something we want. We're fighting for an equal education." The city-suburban school partnership added new hope to that fight (Freire, 1998, 2006).

❖

Next Steps

Whenever we ask what the next step should be, what more we can do to make schools equal, the students always say this: make Metro bigger. "We could expand it," "have more schools join," "get more city schools and suburban schools to work all together." They want Metro to grow, not just with more students, but also with parents, teachers, and anyone else who "cares about how kids are getting taught." That's why this book spends time in two very different schools, listens in on sometimes awkward, cross-community conversations, and stays close to the action for educational equity—to make it easier to imagine doing something similar, and better. This concluding chapter is where I pass the message on, asking readers to follow the Metro students' lead and make movement towards an equal education system.

An overarching goal of this book is to dislodge the apathy that freezes us in the face of a problem-filled world. Seeing what high school students from divided communities can do sparks hopefulness and reveals new possibilities for change.

But it's not vague feel-goods this book is after—*The Metropolitan Community* offers a blueprint drawn in pencil for turning that hope into action. Some of the suggestions are from what was successful about Metro, and some represent learning from when its path bent away from our intentions.

Building a Metro Infrastructure

For educators, youth workers, and community organizers who want to try this at home, the first step is to build an infrastructure for bringing city and suburban students together. This means finding your teacher counterparts in the separate school system and forming connections with community-based advocates. There will be logistics to arrange such as obtaining field trip permissions, securing transportation, reserving meeting space, and purchasing lunches.

Once an intentional and supportive space has been developed, the main tasks will be facilitating understanding, conversation, and action, and identifying what success looks like.

Facilitating Understanding

There is both an experiential and a contextual piece to facilitating students' understanding of educational inequality. What made the biggest difference for the Metro kids was actually being in each other's schools: walking the hallways, sitting in on classes, going to the library, hanging out in the cafeteria. Schools are often big places, and it can be overwhelming to cover so much ground. Multiple trips back and forth can provide a feel for the commonalities and differences between buildings.

As educators though, we need to help students put their observations into context, to add depth and prevent incorrect assumptions from forming. A top-line source of needed information is how schools are funded: what the state's contribution is, how property taxes work, and why that's important. There is also an importance to conveying the "root causes" of school funding inequity, the racialized history and present that underlie these educational disparities. A suggestion from something we missed is to attend to the positionality of this understanding: the responsibility of white and affluent places for the concentration of educational advantage and awareness of

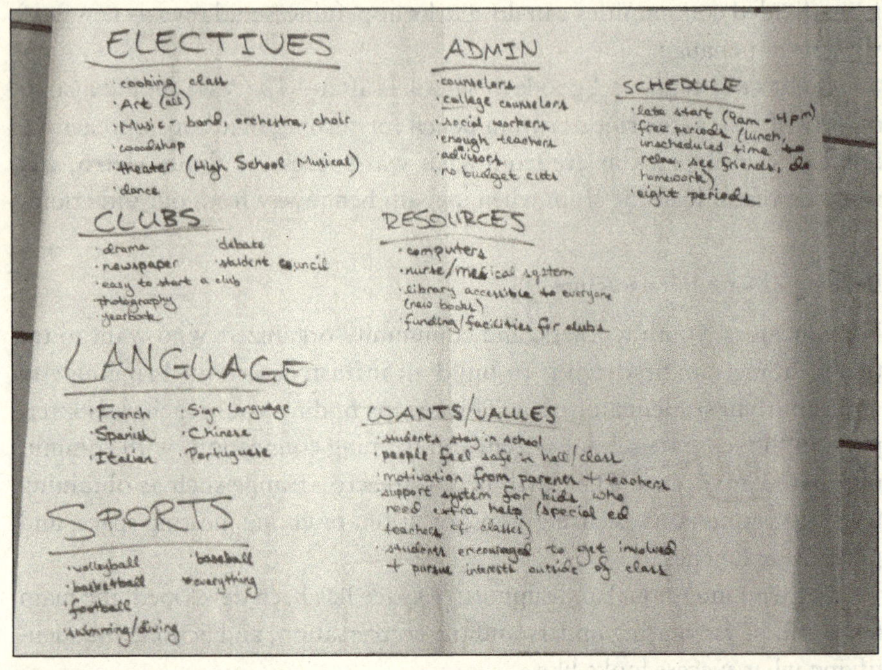

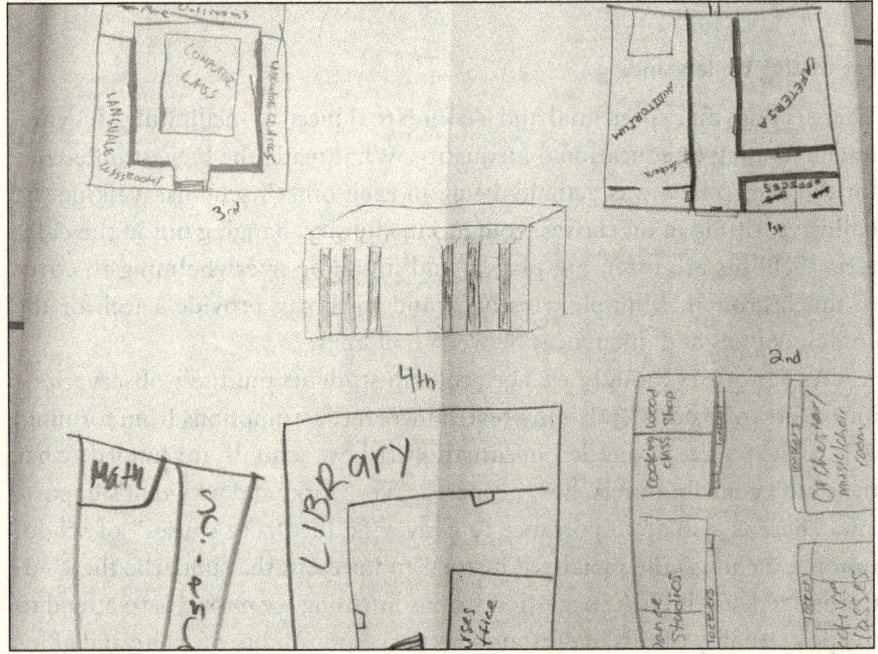

Another dream school, from the Metro students.

the systemic obstacles that strengthen survival muscles but also hinder city schools from thriving.

Facilitating Conversation

From city and suburban students' conversations in *The Metropolitan Community*, educators can anticipate the sticking points and facilitate more authentic communication.

A guiding principle can be to avoid judgment-sounding exhortations to "be honest" and instead encourage students to be "open" and "direct." Another is to expect these conversations to be emotional and know these feelings will vary depending on where students are coming from.

For city students, there will be vulnerability and hurt in schools not having all they need. To comfort these emotions, they can be guided into identifying school strengths too, and away from conflating school needs with personal flaws. Suburban students can be expected to feel guilty or presumed snobby about their school's excess and encouraged to acknowledge advantage without such judgments. In addition, they can be prepared for the legitimate upset city students may feel on seeing their school and view that as systemically, rather than personally, directed. City students need to know it isn't mean to express anger over what the suburban school has—that's not an insult, it comes from a place of wanting resources for their school, too. A practice point for suburban students is expressing how city schools are different while fulfilling their desire to communicate sensitively.

For everyone, discomfort and embarrassment can be accepted as going with the territory for a time. Sustained, year-long interactions, and discussing school differences for the purpose of action, can lessen these feelings and make those that remain seem worth it.

Facilitating Action

The advocacy depicted in *The Metropolitan Community* can offer guidance to educators on how to prepare students for political action.

Many of the tactics of community organizing—door-knocking, giving personal testimony, composing a "story of self," and writing public letters—can be taught and practiced beforehand. Politicians' roles and biographies—their influence in policymaking, their prior record on education-related bills—can be researched to help students see their activism has a specific (and not amorphous) target. Connecting with existing school equity campaigns and reaching out to legislative aides can lay the groundwork for new or continuing "metro"-style actions.

Readying students with workarounds for the dodges of professional politicians will be important preparation for their meetings. And afterwards, celebrating the collaborative effort, debriefing the difficulties, and recognizing the wins will create a culture of activism with the stamina to tackle such an entrenched problem.

Recognizing Successes

Traditionally, the success of activism is measured by policy change, which makes sense because this is the ultimate goal. But change is rarely linear or all-at-once. When supporting new activists, particularly young people sensitive to setbacks, it's necessary to help them see the smaller wins along the way. In *The Metropolitan Community*, some of these wins included breaking out of social isolation, developing solidarity with students on the other side of the line, feeling good about the work to make things better, and—having fun.

The students' initiative to raise awareness within their own communities was also an action success. The suburban students worked on dispelling myths about city schools and countering resistance to change. The city students shared the surprising resources present in the suburban school and funding's role in the disparity.

There were also small victories on the road to legislative action, such as: getting meetings with powerful decision-makers, shaming narrow-interest politics by example, and providing student impact stories to supportive legislators. Which led up to the bigger wins: the votes the Metro students helped persuade in favor of school funding reform.

By elucidating these successes, *The Metropolitan Community* can assist educators in spotlighting their own students' wins, both big and small. The momentum for changing how public schools are funded will be supported in the process.

❖

The Dream

When I began this book, I knew I didn't want to leave you in the worst doldrums, confirming a pessimism that things will never change. You can look almost anywhere around you for that. At the risk of sounding cheesy, I wanted to give you a hope offering, our "dream of a new society:" a metropolitan community (Freire, 1998, p. 74; *Milliken v. Bradley*, 1974, p. 804). It is a dream in the sense that we totally, admittedly, didn't get there—yet—and we are a small project in one Midwestern city. But we did try it with some successes, many times, with real kids and real politicians. We've gained some knowledge, which I've shared with you, on how to do this, and we have some ideas for what to do next. So the metropolitan community is less dreamy than many other dreams. If you pick up your tools now, you won't be starting from scratch, you'll be joining a reality in-the-making.

❖

References

Baker, B. (2018). *Educational inequality and school finance: Why money matters for America's students.* Cambridge, MA: Harvard University Press.

Baker, B., Di Carlo, M. & Green, P. (2022). *School segregation and school funding: How housing discrimination reproduces unequal opportunity.* Albert Shanker Institute.

Baker, B., Srikanth, A., Cotto, R. & Green, P. (2020). School funding disparities and the plight of Latinx children. *Education Policy Analysis Archives, 28*(135): 1–26.

Candelaria, C. & Shores, K. (2019). Court ordered finance reforms in the adequacy era: Heterogeneous causal effects and sensitivity. *Education Finance and Policy, 14*(1): 31–60.

Darling-Hammond, L. (2013). Inequality and school resources: What it will take to close the opportunity gap. In P. Carter & K. Welner (Eds.), *Closing the opportunity gap: What America must do to give every child an even chance.* Oxford: Oxford University Press.

Freire, P. (1998). *Pedagogy of freedom: Ethics, democracy, and civic courage.* Lanham, MD: Rowman & Littlefield.

Freire, P. (2006). *Pedagogy of the oppressed* (30th anniversary ed.). New York, NY: Continuum.

Hyman, J. (2017). Does money matter in the long run? Effects of school spending on educational attainment. *American Economic Journal: Economic Policy, 9*(4): 256–280.

Jackson, C. K. (2020). Does school spending matter? The new literature on an old question. In L. Tach et al. (Eds.), *Confronting inequality: How policies and practices shape children's opportunities.* American Psychological Association.

Jackson, C. K., Johnson, R. & Perisco, C. (2016). The effects of school spending on educational and economic outcomes: Evidence from school finance reforms. *The Quarterly Journal of Economics, 131*: 157–218.

Knight, D., Hassairi, N. & Martinez, D. (2022). Segregation and school funding disparities in California: Contemporary trends 50 years after *Serrano. BYU Law Journal, 1*(6): 1–29.

LaFortune, J., Rothstein, J. & Schazenbach, D. (2018). School finance reform and the distribution of student achievement. *American Economic Journal: Applied Economics, 10*(2): 1–26.

Lichter, D., Thiede, B. & Brooks, M. (2023). Racial diversity and segregation: Comparing principal cities, inner-ring suburbs, outlying suburbs, and the suburban fringe. *RSF Journal of the Social Sciences.* 9(1): 26–51.

Massey, D. (2008). *Categorically unequal: The American stratification system.* New York, NY: Russell Sage.

McGhee, H. (2021). *The sum of us: What racism costs everyone and how we can prosper together.* New York, NY: One World.

Milliken v. Bradley 418 U.S. 717 1974.

Oakes, J. & Rogers, J. (2006). *Learning power: Organizing for education and justice.* New York, NY: Teachers College Press.

Orfield, G. (2013). Housing segregation produces unequal schools: Causes and solutions. In P. Carter & K. Welner (Eds.), *Closing the opportunity gap: What America must do to give every child an even chance.* Oxford: Oxford University Press.

Owens, A. (2023). Separate and unequal: The need for nuanced accounting of the inequalities created by segregation. *Poverty and Race.* 32(2): 9–10.

Owens, A. & Rich, P. (2023). Little boxes all the same? Racial-ethnic segregation and educational inequality across the urban-suburban divide. *RSF Journal of Social Sciences,* 9(2): 26–54.

Roy, J. (2011). Impact of school finance reform on resource equalization and academic performance: Evidence from Michigan. *Education Finance and Policy,* 6(2): 137–167.

Ryan, J. (2010). *Five miles away, a world apart: One city, two schools, and the story of educational opportunity in modern America.* Oxford: Oxford University Press.

Siegal-Hawley, G. (2016). *When the fences come down: Twenty-first century lessons from metropolitan school desegregation.* Chapel Hill, NC: The University of North Carolina Press.

Warren, M. & Mapp, K. (2011). *A match on dry grass: Community organizing as a catalyst for school reform.* Oxford: Oxford University Press.

ACKNOWLEDGMENTS

FIRST AND FOREMOST, I want to express immense gratitude to all the Metro students who ever participated in the project. Your bravery, openness, curiosity, and willingness to work through discomfort created a beautiful partnership. Your activism accomplished real change. Thank you for allowing me to follow you around at school and on field trips, and basically ignoring me while I scribbled notes. Thank you for sharing your impromptu thoughts and for your trust during interviews. This book is dedicated to you.

Huge appreciation for the teachers who co-founded the Metropolitan Community Project with me. Maura, there is no Metro without you. I appreciate your thoughtfulness, your intentionality, your deep knowledge of teaching and the public school system, the amazing sounding-board you provide, and your partnership in beginning this crazy dream. You've challenged me to do better, to think more deeply. Most of all, I am thankful for a dozen years of friendship. Sean, thanks for being willing to add Metro to so many other responsibilities, for your humor, for your co-planning, for welcoming me to your school. It has been wonderful to witness your teaching and deep connection with your students over many years. Thanks also for our summertime decompressions. Tom, thank you for helping me bring your school into Metro and for our talks about history and policy. So glad our friendship continued through career and life changes. Grateful as well to the many other Metro teachers who've participated or assisted over the years—Marlenne, Anna, Wissam, Armando, Michael, Dan, Spiro, Rachel, Anne, Dave, Makoto, and Yosra—and to the principals of "Wyndham" and "Taylor" for hosting us.

Thank you to the organizers of "Northwest Collective" for co-creating Metro and for your sustained partnership. Elena, grateful for the leadership you provided in Metro's first years. Christian, thank you for supporting the Metro students with their school tours and for sharing your organizing strategies with the project. A tidal wave of gratitude to Juliet, the beating heart of Metro. I say that because you moved the project to find its core, "the root of the root" as you always put it, in racial and economic justice. You are the heart in another way, because you center the relational and emotional health of our young activists, alongside the tactics and the policies.

I'd like to thank the Illinois state legislators who met with our Metro students and in my next breath ask you to do more: let's fully fund the evidence-based (needs-based) formula as well as early childhood education in Illinois. How about going even bigger and ending school funding's reliance on property taxes completely? Illinois students, and their families, have been waiting too long for this institution to do the right thing.

I appreciate my academic mentors and professors who sent me on this path: Carla O'Connor at the University of Michigan-Ann Arbor and Michael Fultz, Stacey Lee, Mary Metz, and Bill Reese at the University of Wisconsin-Madison.

Thanks to my friends and my sister for helping me with the writing and publishing side of this book: Kat for your help with revisions and insights into the world of publishing, plus the Residency on the Farm space to write; Sarah R. for your cheerleading of this project, your longstanding friendship, and your suggestion of Myers Education Press; Emmy for helping me think through the Metro students' metaphors; Paula for being a project booster and grounded friend; Holly for strategizing about emails to publishers and checking my grammar.

To the team at Myers Education Press, particularly Chris and Stephanie, I appreciate all your work in giving *The Metropolitan Community* an outlet. Appreciation as well to Eve, for copyediting.

To Rachel, Jay, Avi, Syd, Maura, Larry, Santi, Alejandro, Tina, Marc, and John, thanks for being family in my adopted home.

To my homegrown family—Holly, Alec, Liam, Stu, Sarah T., Zoe, Jack, Mom, and Dad—thank you for supporting this book and your belief in me. How many times did I hear, "What's happening with your book?," a question holding certainty that there would, eventually, be a happening. Here it is! Love you lots.

The Metropolitan Community Project is a collaborative effort, but all mistakes and omissions in this book are mine. I tried in these pages to do the Metro kids, and their city and suburban high schools, justice. I know I have more work to do. We all do, if we're going to get to the end of the educational divide. Here's to creating many metropolitan communities, in reality. I'm here for the next steps.

❖

METRO DIRECTORY[1]

TAYLOR HIGH SCHOOL[2]

Chicago public "neighborhood" (non-selective) high school

Students:
(in order of appearance)

Andy
Lena
Anna
Angelica
Trina
Jerry
Papi
Lali
Mia
Bianca
Xavia
Alex
Janelle
Kenny
Rusty
Alexandria
Moe
Lucy
Allie
Mario
Ailany
Slim
Katie
Celia
Elani
Corey
Maria
Jaime
Kaycey
Rosa
Denise
Ben
Keke
Eddy
Anthony
David

Teachers:
(in order of appearance)

Ms. Dorsey
Mr. Ryan

WYNDHAM HIGH SCHOOL[3]

Suburban public "neighborhood" (non-selective) high school

Students:

(in order of appearance)

Caroline
Shana
Maggie
Amanda
Jade
Jashaundra
Brian
Noa
Abbey
Haley
Matt
Zoe
Simone
Eve
Claire
Kylie
Caitlin
Maya
Adrianna
Jonas
Annaliese
Elizabeth
Lisa
Laila
Betty
Jonathan
Sarah
Olivia
Prem
Ruth

Teachers:

(in order of appearance)

Mr. Bartel

NORTHWEST COLLECTIVE

Nonprofit, community-based organization in northwest Chicago (Taylor High School's neighborhood), which advocates for immigration, housing, labor, voting, and education rights.

Community Organizers:

(in order of appearance)

Ms. Isabel
Mr. Rafael
Ms. Sofia

ILLINOIS STATE LEGISLATURE[4]

Elected state office-holders who met with the Metro students

Metro State Legislators:

(in order of appearance)

Senator Joseph Bauer	*Democrat*	Suburban district
House Representative Claire Orlov	*Democrat*	Suburban district
House Representative Patrick Knight	*Democrat*	Chicago district
Senator Sonya Cowan	*Democrat*	Chicago and suburban district
House Representative Michelle Reyes	*Democrat*	Chicago and suburban district
House Representative Ed Miske	*Democrat*	Chicago and suburban district
Senator Vanessa Schneider	*Republican*	Suburban district
Senator Laurie Irving	*Democrat*	Suburban district
Senator Dave Lewin	*Democrat*	Rural district
House Representative Ron Griffiths	*Republican*	Rural district

Notes

1. All school, community organization, student, teacher, organizer, and legislator names in this book and directory are pseudonyms, to protect the identities of Metropolitan Community Project participants.
2. More Taylor students and teachers participated in Metro than are listed here; this directory includes participants who are quoted in the book to help identify their school and city affiliation in the text.
3. More Wyndham students and teachers participated in Metro than are listed here; this directory includes participants who are quoted in the book to help identify their school and suburban affiliation in the text.
4. The Illinois State Legislature is the actual institution the Metro students engaged with, and its name has not been changed. The Metro students met with more state legislators than are listed here, particularly while advocating in Springfield, the state capitol. This directory includes legislators who are quoted in the book to help identify their chamber, party, and district affiliation in the text.

ABOUT THE AUTHOR

CYNTHIA TAINES is a sociologist of education who is fascinated by students' perspectives about school and their actions for educational equality. She has published in highly regarded academic journals, including the *American Educational Research Journal, The Journal of Educational Change, Education and Urban Society, Teachers College Record*, and *The Urban Review*. With teachers and organizers, Cynthia co-founded the Metropolitan Community Project, a city-suburban partnership for educational justice. She is an Associate Professor in the College of Education at Northern Illinois University and holds a Ph.D. in Educational Policy Studies, with minors in Sociology and History, from the University of Wisconsin-Madison. Cynthia resides in Chicago.

INDEX

Note: all Metro participant names are pseudonyms

A
abundance, 47–48, 51, 77, 146, 167, 184, 191
achievement gaps, 3, 103, 154–158, 166
activism. *See* student activism
advocacy. *See* student activism
affluence, 4–6, 13, 54, 192, 195
alienation, 158–160
Alinsky, Saul, 154, 177–178
altruism, 175–178
apathy, 4–5, 167, 191–193, 196–197
attendance obstacles, 25, 157–158
awareness building, 143–149, 163–171, 178–179, 183–184

B
Bauer, Joseph (State Legislator IL-D), 91–92, 192, 211
box metaphor, 144–145, 164
'bragging,' 47–50, 65, 67
Brown v. Board (1954), 8–9
bubble metaphor, 163–165, 167–168, 178–179, 183

C
charter schools, 7
Chávez, César, 19
cities, 4–5, 7–8, 12, 14, 22, 29, 65, 79–80, 83–84, 143–145, 147, 150–151, 154, 157–159, 164, 176, 194–195, 210
  box, 144–145, 164
  educational divide and, 4, 13–14, 124, 169, 176
  political power, 5, 110, 114, 176, 194–195, 210
city-suburban school partnership, 5, 8–9, 14–15, 38, 72, 87, 107, 111–112, 114, 134–135, 151–152, 159, 174–175, 178–179, 185, 191, 193–196, 201
class sizes, 19, 30–31, 84, 103, 194
classism. *See* politics of advantage
college access, 19–20, 27, 29–30, 33, 46, 52–55, 61–65, 73, 91–92, 97, 103, 105, 107, 120–121, 155, 158, 164, 167
common good. *See* solidarity
communicating the divide
  dimming down inequality, 43, 45–47, 51–54, 62–65, 69–71, 77–79
  direct talk, 51, 67–69, 79, 81, 85, 87, 199
  discomforts, 43, 47–51, 54–56, 59–61, 65–67, 71–74, 77–79
  emotional work, 49–50, 54–56, 59–60, 65–67, 73–74, 77–79, 199
  'honesty' and, 51, 55–56, 67–69, 78–79, 81–84, 199
  'open' communication, 43, 51, 67–69, 79–87, 199
community-based organizing, 5, 11, 16*n3*, 86, 91–93, 96–99, 100–107, 110–114, 117–122, 125, 128–129, 177–178, 194, 199–200, 205–206, 210
'complaining,' 73, 153–154, 176, 185
Cowan, Sonya (State Legislator IL-D), 104–107, 110, 192, 211
critical consciousness, 143–149, 158–159, 167–171, 183–184, 196
  See also Freire, Paulo

D
demographics
  city schools, 4–5, 7–8, 14
  legislative districts, 110–111, 118, 135, 164, 174, 176, 195
  suburban schools, 7, 9, 163
'deserving' equality, 48, 109, 115, 122, 148, 184–185
Día de los Muertos, 24

direct communication, 51, 67–69, 79, 81, 85, 87, 199
directory of Metro participants, 16*n3*, 209–211
discrimination, 119, 158, 169
    See also politics of advantage
disparities. *See* educational inequality

E
educational activism. *See* student activism
educational divide
    communication about, 43, 45–56, 59–74, 77–87, 199
    history of, 4, 8–9, 12–14, 169, 197
    politics of, 4–5, 12–14, 124, 169, 172–173, 176–178, 185, 191–192
    school funding and, 3–6, 11–14, 25, 86, 92–93, 97–100, 106, 113, 128–129, 172, 192, 197, 206
educational equality, vii, 3, 8–9, 12, 38, 50, 72, 78, 85, 98–99, 104–106, 111, 121–122, 128–129, 147–149, 151, 154, 157, 170–171, 173, 175–176, 178–179, 193–196, 206
    and reform bill success, 128–129, 195–196
educational inequality, 3–8, 11–14, 65, 69, 78–79, 81, 84–86, 93, 98, 104, 111, 119, 134, 143, 145–147, 152–154, 156–159, 166–169, 172, 174, 176–179, 185, 191–193, 195, 197–200
educational opportunity, 6, 8–9, 14, 38, 46, 48–50, 53, 59, 72, 74, 77, 81, 84, 86, 99, 104, 121–122, 143, 148, 150, 153–154, 158, 166–168, 170–172, 174, 184–185
    obstacles, 4, 54, 63–65, 78, 85, 145–148, 150, 157–158, 167, 184, 192, 199
embarrassment, 47–48, 67, 74, 77, 133, 199
empathy, 5, 68, 93, 104, 123, 163–166, 171, 174, 183
'envy,' 72–74
exclusion, 4, 13–14, 163, 171

F
fear of causing offense, 43, 50, 52–53, 55–56, 72–74, 77–79, 83, 199
fear of judgment, 43, 47–48, 51, 56, 59–62, 64–68, 74, 77–79, 81–82, 97, 99, 120, 153–155, 185, 199
freedom of movement, 20–21, 26, 35, 55, 72, 164
Freire, Paulo, 5, 14, 134, 148, 183–184, 190, 193, 196, 201
funding. *See* school funding

G
Griffiths, Ron (State Legislator IL-R), 128
guilt, 48–51, 86–87, 178, 199

H
hallway interactions, 19, 23–26, *24*, 32, 34–35, 46, 50, 53, 61, 65–66, 168, 197
'honest' communication, 51, 55–56, 67–69, 78–79, 81–84, 199
hopelessness, 4–5, 99, 112, 133, 191–193, 196
    and new hope, 5, 8, 14–15, 190, 193–197, 201
human rights, 9, 11, 99–100, 111, 148, 173, 210

I
immigrant experience, 4, 7, 32, 111, 113, 143, 158, 210
income disparity
    lower-income, 3–5, 7–8, 12–13, 143
    political representation, 4–5, 114, 135, 176, 191–192
    upper-income, 4–5, 80, 145, 169–170, 191–192
individualism, 92, 98, 149, 156–158
    See also meritocracy
injustice, 65, 68, 73–74, 78, 145–146, 158–159, 175, 183
    See also unfairness
Irving, Laurie (State Legislator IL-D), 117–126, 211

K
Knight, Patrick (State Legislator IL-D), 100–104, 211
Kozol, Jonathan, 121

L
legislative districts, 110–111, 118, 135, 164, 174, 176, 195
legislators (See note 130*n1*: all names are pseudonyms)
- Bauer, Joseph (IL-D), 91–92, 192, 211
- Cowan, Sonya (IL-D), 104–107, 110, 192, 211
- Griffiths, Ron (IL-R), 128
- Irving, Laurie (IL-D), 117–126, 211
- Knight, Patrick (IL-D), 100–104, 211
- Lewin, Dave (IL-D), 128
- Miske, Ed (IL-D), 112–114, 192, 194, 211
- Orlov, Claire (IL-D), 97–99, 211
- Reyes, Michelle (IL-D), 110–112, 192, 211
- Schneider, Vanessa (IL-R), 117–121, 125–126, 211

letter samples, 94–95, 101–102, 108–109, 115–116
letter writing campaign, 86, 92–97, 172
Lewin, Dave (State Legislator IL-D), 128
libraries, 21, 34–35, 45, 55, 66, *69*, 70, 84, 97, 100, 103, 105, 148
limits, 12, 52, 54, 63, 66, 89, 91, 120, 147–149, 154, 165, 184
- *See also* Freire, Paulo

local funding, 3–4, 11–13, 107, 134, 170
'luck,' 169–170, 172

M
Marshall, Thurgood, 8–9, 13, 201
meritocracy, 72, 78, 92, 121, 143–144, 156
metropolitan community, meaning, 5–6, 8–9, 193–195
- *See also* city-suburban school partnership

Metropolitan Community Project
- background, 5–9
- creation of, 9
- directory of participants, 16*n3*, 209–211
- educational activism, 11, 84–87, 91–129, 133–135, 194–196
- facilitating processes, 197–200
- facilitators
  - community organizers, 9–10, 63, 72, 91–93, *96*, 144, 152, 158, 169, 178, 197, 205–206, 210
  - professor (author), 9–10, 96–97, 104, 106, 117, 124, 197, 205–206, 213
  - teachers, 9–10, *55*, *59*, 63, 66, 70–72, 93, 96–99, 112–114, 117, 122, 178, 197, 205, 209–210
- funding reform success, 128–129, 195–196, 200
- images, *21, 24, 28, 33, 35, 38, 69, 123, 127, 198*
- letter-writing campaign, 86, 92–97, 172
- next steps, 74, 81, 153–154, 157–158, 178–179, 185, 196–201
- policy outcomes, 124–125, 128–129, 195–196, 200
- preparation for action, 10–11, 86, 91–93, 96–97, 104, 112–113, 117, 128, 152, 197–200
- resource equity goal, 72, 92–93
- schools, 6–8
- school tours, 19–38
- student navigators, 51, 67–69
- student outcomes
  - Taylor, 143–159, 183–185, 196
  - Wyndham, 163–179, 183–185, 196
- timespan, 10–11, 81–84, 125, 128–129, 135, 199
- yearly activities, 10–11

Milliken v. Bradley (1974), 8–9, 13, 201, *202n*
Miske, Ed (State Legislator IL-D), 112–114, 192, 194, 211

N
neighborhood schools, 4, 7, 65, 154, 209
normalcy of inequality, 5, 14, 28, 49, 91–92, 108, 134, 146–150, 158–159, 165, 167–168, 183–184, 191–193, 196
See also Freire, Paulo
nurses, 28, 36, 47, 91, 115, 194

O
obstacles, 4, 54, 63–65, 78, 85, 145–148, 150, 157–158, 167, 184, 192, 199
recognition of, 68–69, 84, 143–149, 163–171, 178–179, 183–184
open communication, 43, 51, 67–69, 79–87, 199
and direct talk, 51, 67–69, 79, 81, 85, 87, 199
Orlov, Claire (State Legislator IL-D), 97–99, 211

P
partnership. *See* school partnerships
Police Department, Chicago, 25, 70
politics of advantage, 4–5, 12–14, 92, 100, 110–111, 113–114, 119, 121, 124–125, 134–135, 145, 164, 169, 172–173, 175–179, 184–185, 191–192, 194–195, 197
political inaction, 5, 92, 98, 107, 11, 113–114, 124–125, 133–134, 192
privilege, 47–51, 56, 77, 81, 83, 85–86, 92, 100, 113–114, 119, 124–125, 134–135, 145, 147, 153, 157, 163–165, 167–173, 175–179, 184–185, 191–192, 194–195, 197
as tool for good, 85–86, 119, 125, 135, 153, 167, 170–171, 175, 178–179, 184–185, 194–195
bubble, 163–165, 167–168, 178–179, 183
property taxes, 4, 11–13, 93, 106, 113, 170, 172, 192, 197, 206

R
racism, 4–5, 8–9, 12–14, 52, 59, 110, 169, 135, 157–158, 175–176, 197
See also politics of advantage
Reyes, Michelle (State Legislator IL-D), 110–112, 192, 211

S
Savage Inequalities: Children in America's Schools (Kozol), 121, 130
scarcity, 12, 28, 55, 62, 165
Schneider, Vanessa (State Legislator IL-R), 117–121, 125–126, 211
school district boundaries, 3–4, 7–9, 13, 60, 96–98, 100, 111–114, 117–118, 124, 169, 211
school funding
effects of, 3, 103, 155–158, 166, 191
federal funding, 11–12
local funding, 3–4, 11–13, 107, 134, 170
needs-based funding, 3, 12, 98, 113, 121, 124, 128–129, 170, 195–196, 200, 206
property taxes, 4, 11–13, 93, 106, 113, 170, 172, 192, 197, 206
reform bill, 128–129, 195–196, 200
state funding, 11–12, 25, 86, 92–93, 97–100, 107, 117, 125, 128, 193–196, 206
school partnerships, 5, 8–9, 14–15, 38, 72, 87, 107, 111–112, 114, 134–135, 151–152, 159, 174–175, 178–179, 185, 191, 193–196, 201
school resources, 4–6, 11, 73–74, 194
architecture and grounds, 6–7, 37, 45–47, 68, 71, 106
art classes, 4, 19, *33*, 37, 47, 55, 61, 63, 70, 72, 168
class sizes, 19, 30–31, 37, 84, 103, 194
college counseling/college access, 19–20, 27, 29–30, 33, 46, 52–55, 61–65, 73, 91–92, 95, 97, 103, 105, 107–109, 115, 120–121, 155, 158, 164, 167
community feel, 23, 34–35, 46, 50, 52–53, 59–62, 65–66, 77, 149, 158
cooking classes, 30, 94
discipline, 7, 26–27, 61–62, 64, 66–67
electives, 31, 33, 45, 50, 60, 71, 80, 153, 168

English classes, 28–29, 31–32, 45, 70, 98
field trips, 28, 31–32, 122
freedom of movement, 20–21, 26, 35, 55, 72, 164
history classes, 30–31, 70
libraries, 21, 34–35, 45, 55, 66, *69*, 70, 84, 94, 97, 100, 103, 105, 148, 194
military training/JROTC, 27, *28*, 52, 63, 66
murals and culture, 19, 23, *24*, 25, 52–53, 60–61, 63, 65–66, 77, 149, 194
music/band classes, 22–23, 32, 51, 55, 61–62
nurses, 28, 36, 47, 91, 115, 194
physical education/gyms, 21–22, 36–37, 45, 47, 48–49, 70–72, 52–53, 80, 94, 105–106, 153
police/security guards, 7, 20, 23, 25–27, 35, 64, 66–67, 70, 94
radio station, 30, 43, 167
school lunch, 7, 20–21, 38, 45, 60, 63–64, 66–67, 70
science classes, 20, *55*, 73, 194
supplies, 20, 28–29, 34, 55, 63, 86, 96
swimming pool, 22, 37, 43, 56
teachers/teacher access, 28–31, 35–36, 53, 60–64, 98, 118–119, 149, 153, 167
technology, 4, 24, 31, 34, 47, 55, 62, 72–73, 97, 103, 105, 108–109 153, 156
world language classes, 23–25, 52, 63, 66, 80
segregation, 3–9, 12–14, 111, 143, 157, 163–164, 169, 173, 193
See also educational divide
separate worlds/same world, 143–146, 152–153, 163–166, 168–169, 176–178, 185
shame, 74, 77, 87, 199
social safety net, 29, 92, 102, 157, 165, 167
solidarity, 4–5, 8, 85–86, 143, 150–154, 158–159, 170–171, 174–179, 185, 191, 193–201
See also city-suburban school partnership
Springfield (state capitol), 86, *96*, 122–125, *123*, 127–128, 211*n4*
standardized testing, 53, 60, 93, 105, 155, 158
state funding, 11–12, 25, 86, 92–93, 97–100, 107, 117, 125, 128, 193–196, 206
funding reform, 113, 121, 124, 128–129, 195–196, 200
meetings with state legislators, 91–92, 97–122, 128–129
stereotypes, 59, 66–67, 78, 120, 155, 173
student activism
letter samples, 94–95, 101–102, 108–109, 115–116
letter writing strategy, 86, 92–97, 172
meetings with state legislators, *96*–124, *123, 127, 129*, 194–199
open communication and, 84–87
policy outcomes, 124–125, 128–129, 195–196, 200
preparation for, 10–11, 86, 91–93, 96–97, 104, 112–113, 117, 128, 197–200
school funding reform bill, 128–129, 195–196, 200
strategies/tactics, 11, 86, 91–93, 96–99, 100–107, 110–114, 117–122, 125, 128–129, 173–174, 199–200
student-led, 10–11, 92–93
student outcomes, 149–151, 171–174, 184–185, 196
student reflections on, 85–87, 99–100, 104, 110, 112, 114, 122–127, 196
ups and downs of, 133–135
suburbs, 3–7, 12–14, 20, 32, 46, 48, 54, 56, 72, 80, 83, 85, 92, 100, 105–107, 110–111, 113–114, 119, 124–125, 134–135, 145, 153, 157, 163–165, 168–170, 172–179, 191–192, 194–195, 197
bubble, 163–165, 167–168, 178–179, 183

educational divide and, 3–5, 8–9, 12–14, 56, 72, 92, 106–107, 111, 113–114, 119, 124–125, 134, 145, 153, 157, 168–170, 172–179, 185, 191–192, 197
increased options, 72, 92–93, 121–122, 157, 172
political power, 4–5, 12–14, 92, 100, 110–111, 113–114, 119, 121, 124–125, 134–135, 145, 164, 169, 172–173, 175–179, 184–185, 191–192, 194–195, 197
surveillance, 7, 20, 23, 26–27, 64, 67, 70, 168–169
survivors, 156–158, 199

T
Taylor High School (Chicago)
architecture and grounds, 7, 106
art classes, 4, 19, 55, 61, 63
assets, 5, 19, 23–25, 28–29, 34, 54, 59–63, 65–66, 144–145, 149–151, 154, 158, 184–185, 194, 199–200
attendance obstacles, 25, 158–159
background, 5–8
band/music classes, 22–23, 51, 55, 61–62
box metaphor, 144–145, 164
bravery, 78, 84, 99–100, 106–107, 118, 120, 185
class sizes, 19, 84, 103, 194
college access and guidance, 19–20, 27, 29–30, 52–55, 60–63, 65, 73, 91–92, 97, 103, 105, 107, 155, 120
communicating the divide, 43
presenting Taylor, 59–69, 77–79
reactions to Wyndham, 69–74, 77–79
open communication, 67–69, 79–87, 199
community feel, 23, 52–53, 59–62, 65–66, 149, 158
'complaining,' 73, 153–154, 176, 185
'deserve' equality, 109, 122, 148, 184–185
discipline, 7, 26–27, 61–62, 64, 66–67
electives, 60, 80
English classes, 28–29, 98
'envy,' 72–74
field trips, 28, 122
freedom of movement, 20–21, 26, 55
history classes, 31
images from, *21, 24, 28*
library, 21, 55, 66, 84, 94, 97, 100, 103, 105, 148
military/ROTC, 27–28, 52, 63, 66
murals and culture, 19, 23, *24*, 25, 52–53, 60–61, 63, 65–66, 77, 149, 194
nurses, 28, 36, 47, 91, 194
outcomes of Metro project, 143–159, 183–185, 196
physical education/gyms, 21–22, 52–53, 105–106
police/security guards, 7, 20, 23, 25–27, 64, 66–67
school lunch, 7, 20–21, 60, 63–64, 66–67, 70
science classes, 20, 55, 194
shame, 74, 77, 87, 199
supplies, 20, 28–29, 55, 63, 86
swimming pool, 22, 56
teachers/teacher access, 28–29, 36, 52–53, 60–64, 98, 118–119, 149
technology, 4, 24, 55, 62, 72–73, 97, 103, 105, 156
tour of, 19–29
world language classes, 23–25, 52, 66
teachers, 28–31, 35–36, 53, 60–64, 98, 118–119, 149, 153, 167
substitute teachers, 61–62, 64, 98

U
'unaffected' by inequality, 119–20, 128, 141, 152–154, 156–157, 166, 168–170, 175–179, 185, 197–199
unfairness, 50, 54, 72–74, 85, 119, 122, 134, 146–148, 176, 183
See also educational inequality

W

wealth and whiteness. *See* politics of advantage
Wyndham High School (suburbs)
architecture and grounds, 6, 37, 45–47, 68, 71
art classes, 4, 33, 37, 47, 70, 72, 168
assets, 5, 85–86, 96, 107, 119, 123–125, 134–135, 151–153, 170–175, 177–179, 184–185, 194–195, 200
background, 5–7
band/music classes, 22, 32
'bragging,' 47–50, 65, 67
bubble metaphor, 163–165, 167–168, 178–179, 183
class sizes, 19, 30–31, 37, 103
college access and guidance, 30, 33, 46, 54, 73, 91–92, 103, 105, 155, 164, 167–168, 194
communicating the divide, 43
presenting Wyndham, 45–51, 77–79
reactions to Taylor, 51–56, 77–79
open communication, 51, 79–87, 199
community feel, 34–35, 46, 50, 52–53, 61–62
cooking classes, 30
discipline, 27, 62
downsides, 19, 33–34, 36, 46, 48, 50, 53–54, 163–165, 177–179
electives, 31, 33, 45, 50, 71, 80, 153, 168
English classes, 31–32, 45, 70
field trips, 31–32, 122
freedom of movement, 21, 26, 35, 72, 164
guilt, 48–51, 86–87, 178, 199
history classes, 30–31, 70, 194
images from, *33*, *35*, *69*
library, 34–35, *35*, 45, 70, 84, 97, 100, 105, 194
'luck,' 169–170, 172
military/ROTC, 27, 52
nurses, 36, 47, 194
outcomes of Metro project, 163–179, 183–185, 196
physical education/gyms, 36–37, 45, 47–48, 70–72, 80, 105–106
police/security guards, 35, 70
privilege as tool for good, 85–86, 119, 125, 135, 153, 167, 170–171, 175, 178–179, 184–185, 194–195
radio station, 30, 43, 167
school lunch, 38, 45, 70
science classes, 11, 20, 73
supplies, 34, 96
swimming pool, 37, 43
teachers/teacher access, 11, 30–31, 35–36, 118, 167
technology, 24, 31, 34, 47, 72, 105, 153
tour of, 30–38
world language classes, 23–24, 52, 63, 80